THE GOSPEL FACTOR

The Preaching in Revival

Michael Livengood

"As a young revivalist, I can only speak from my perspective; I found this book is full of wisdom, both experiential from Michael's life and Divine, from the heart of God. The first third is full of nuggets of gold for anyone wanting to pursue evangelism, revival, or pastor their people in a more refined and fruitful way, while the second two-thirds are personal sermons from the fires of actual revivals that Michael has been in. You will hear the Holy Spirit on every page, whispering to you, "This is the way; walk ye in it." It is so crucial in our day that we keep passing the baton of revival—its history, its language, and its culture—to the next generation, lest we simmer into the lukewarmth of religious Sunday practices and nominal Christianity. Whether you are starting out, in the mid-life of ministry, or leaving a legacy, you will be writing down the quotes and notes almost as fast as you read them. I have felt the fine scalpel of Doctor Jesus as I read, cutting away the excess and unnecessary things that stop me from being that fine-tuned and polished vessel, ready for the Master's use. Thank you for pouring out your heart, Michael, the true heart of an Evangelist."

Joseph Lee, Revivalist, Pioneer Ministry, Auckland, New Zealand

"In his latest book, Michael gives you opportunity to learn, grow and develop in your preaching. This is drawn from his extensive experience in evangelistic and revival preaching in local churches and extended moves of God.

Michael ministers cross-denominationally, as well as cross-culturally. I have seen Michael bring focus and intentionality to many preachers and evangelists over the years. The principles he shares are simple, yet profound.

Having had the privilege of standing alongside Michael in hundreds of revival services, I have seen God use him to harvest, disciple and equip thousands. I encourage you to receive not just information, but an impartation from this book, as Michael shares his journey to no more fruitless meetings."

Dr. Seth Fawcet, Apostolic Leader, Hope Network International

"Michael Livengood is a powerful and valued representative of the New Testament church. His book, *The Gospel Factor — The Preaching in Revival,* is a master class textbook on the art and science of preaching! The church needs this book, as we must return to strong biblical preaching, with an emphasis on the altar. Michael's teaching on the importance of and difference in preaching between the Evangelistic/Revivalist and a Pastor is something that every pastor should read and understand."

Phil Schneider, Superintendent of the Illinois Assembly of God

"In his latest book, evangelist Michael Livengood explores the importance of preaching. Having been a hearer and recipient of many well-timed sermons preached by Michael, I highly value his insight into this all-important aspect of ministry and of revival. In this book, he does not disappoint. *The Gospel Factor* is filled with spiritual and practical insights that will encourage and strengthen each reader, whether or not the reader has ever had the opportunity to preach the gospel in a formal manner. I encourage everyone to add this book to their library for both personal enrichment and as a ministry resource."

Rodney Burton, Evangelist (Rodney Burton Ministries)

"*The Gospel Factor* is not hyperbole or platitudes. This book is a practical guide on how to evangelize the world through solid biblical preaching. *The Gospel Factor* should be a part of the curriculum of every serious student of revival. It is chock full of powerful stories and anecdotes for the reader. Bravo to *The Gospel Factor!*"

Randall Burton, Pastor, Northview Church, Columbus, IN

"A preachers handbook, but not only that...an instructional, inspirational, reflationary, practical, experiential, and anointed masterpiece which comes out of Michael Livengood's heart of integrity...no smoke and mirrors, but real and raw truth he and Linda have experienced.

The Gospel Factor — *the Preaching of Revival* gives clear understanding of the both/and of revival preaching and evangelism, as well as tips as to how this can be a reality in revival. It clearly delineates the difference between revivals and Godsent revival, between revival and evangelism.

Within these pages is expository evidence of power preaching for and in Revival, gleaned from 25 plus years of experiencing this God phenomenon.

Advice, if heeded, in this book could save revival preachers from falling into a hole and missing some of the amazing things God has for them and for his glory. Read slowly, check out scripture in relation to your reading, allow the Holy Spirit to speak...and He will. Here is a tool sanctioned by Him which will provide answers you may have long sought."

Colleen Doyle, 'Go Ministries International, New Zealand

"*The Gospel Factor*. I want you to read this book. Seriously, if you are one of those that are genuine GOD chasers, you need to read it. If you are not a God chaser who hungers desperately for another move of God that can transform a nation, you also need to read this book. Michael is a friend, a very close one, and a co-worker in the Kingdom of God. He is the real deal. He is speaking out of a place of authority. A place of having walked the talk and has firsthand experience of what he is sharing. In this, his finest work in the *Factor* series, he clearly lays out the keys that will position God's people to be able to catch the unforced rhythms of God's grace. Well done, my friend, my brother-in-arms. He who has an ear, let him hear what the spirit of the Lord is saying. Love and blessings."

Graham Renouf, Prophet, Pastor, Husband, Father, Grandfather, and Friend

"Michael, I have just finished reading your draft and I must say it is without a doubt, classic Michael Livengood. Your heart and, clearly, very anointed passion to weave practical mechanics, with a strong emphasis on keeping the word of God a bedrock and steadfast foundation with pinpoint direction and balanced with life stories and illustrations under the leading and guidance of the Holy Spirit, is a total package that this book brings to the table. Your heart comes forth as one reads through each chapter; they set a very clear path to help the reader understand and be challenged to better their way to communicate the greatest story to be told.

Thank you for sharing with us examples and illustrations that have been tested and refined in your ministry; many will be blessed, and courage for your gift to the five-fold and the body of Christ."

Keith Taylor, Senior Pastor Cross Tabernacle, Terra Haute, Indiana, member Of the executive leadership of Indiana Assemblies of God, and is recognized as an Apostolic leader by others.

"Just finished your book. Great job, Brother...this is a great addition to the other *Factor* books. The front-end is loaded with clearly-understood insights and steps. The second part of the book provides a great selection of your sermons, which not only illustrate what you previously recommended, they also speak as standalone messages. I can see preachers and evangelists from around the nations adding it to their library being underlined, highlighted and referenced."

Tony Collis, Pastor at Hope Centre, Levin, New Zealand, former director of OAC, a ministry raising up and training evangelists in New Zealand.

MICHAEL LIVENGOOD

THE
GOSPEL
FACTOR

THE PREACHING
IN REVIVAL

THE GOSPEL FACTOR
the preaching in revival

Copyright © 2022 — Michael Livengood

All scripture is taken from the King James Version unless otherwise stated.

ISBN: 9798417294198

B&B PUBLISHING GROUP

FOREWORD

I have known Michael for more than 30 years and in that time, having ministered alongside of Michael in Revival here in the US and abroad, I have heard many of Michael's sermons and stories and have read several of his books, yet I have never been more stirred than by this book, *The Gospel Factor!* I wish a book such as this would have been available when I first started out in ministry as a pastor and especially as an evangelist!

In this book, Michael picks up where our Bible training in hermeneutics, homiletics, and pedagogics left off as he delves into teaching the importance of revival preaching. Michael is a revivalist whose focus is on bringing in the harvest. Concerning his approach to preaching, he states in chapter two, "From start to finish I am going after the harvest. I start the altar call when I start preaching."

There is so much to glean from this book that to describe it all would require me to write a book! In this book he speaks on the need for balance in our worship and preaching, repentance preaching, followed up with discipleship preaching and the emphasis that must be in revival preaching with the main emphasis being SSP: Salvation, Sanctification and Presence, along with keeping the "Main Thing, The Main Thing!" As he states, "Jesus is the Message, the evangelist is the messenger!"

There is in depth teaching on the four types of people at revivals and how preaching to those who have never heard the Gospel is very different from preaching to those who have the Bible memorized!

Bottom line! This book is a manual, and it is a must have for every Pastor, Teacher, and especially every Evangelist aka Revivalist, which we all should be! There is so much more I can say about this book; however, the highlight of this book is the last ten chapters, which are ten sermons that Michael has preached all over the world. What is so special about these sermons is that in each one you see the application of what he has just finished teaching in the previous chapters!

Fredrick Aguilar
Fire On The Altar Ministries
Zion, Illinois

CONTENTS

AUTHOR'S INTRODUCTION

What do you think of when you think of revival? Would I be too far off to suggest that probably your mind went to great atmospheres...awesome music... powerful altar services? All of these are a part of revival. And I love every one of them.

But revival is more than sing...shout...and dance about!

Great preaching is also a part of revival. In this book I want to address that aspect.

We are told in Romans 10:17 that *faith cometh by hearing and hearing by the Word of God.* Faith for salvation comes as people hear the preaching of God's Word. Faith for healing comes as people hear the preaching of God's Word. Faith for the baptism in the Holy Spirit comes as people hear the preaching of God's Word. Need I say more?

My life was impacted by the great revival that took place at the Brownsville Assembly of God in Pensacola, Florida. The preaching of Evangelist Steve Hill was a huge part of that revival.

The worship led by Lindell Cooley was something that needed to be experienced. Within moments of his beginning to lead the worship I would often feel it was already worth the fourteen-or-so-hour drive I had completed to reach the revival.

The altar services were extraordinary. I not only listened to testimonies of incredible encounters with God when hands were laid on people, but I had my own story to add to that mix. Those altar services were probably the reason many, if not most, of the people had waited all day long in the hot Florida sun to get a seat in that building.

1

Having said that, though, Brownsville would not have been Brownsville without the nightly preaching of the Gospel. Conviction fell during the preaching. People would run to the place of repentance when the invitation was given.

In this book I want to address the role of preaching in revival. This is book three in a series. In *The Glory Factor* I wrote on the role of the Glory in revival. In *The Wow Factor* I shared those things we do that attract the manifest Presence of God. In this book I hope to unpackage the importance of revival preaching and what it looks like.

The first part of this book will focus on why the preaching is such an important part. The second part of the book will include a sample of messages I have preached during revivals.

SECTION ONE

WHY PREACHING IS SO IMPORTANT IN REVIVAL

CHAPTER TITLES

CHAPTER ONE

The Focus of Revival Preaching

Spirit vs. Truth in Revival?

I had been invited to preach the Northern Luzon District Prayer Conference of the Assemblies of God in Baguio, Philippines. It was an honor to be invited by both our missionary family and the leadership of the Filipino church. But to be honest, the first two nights of the conference had basically been rather dead and dry. To be sure, 40 to 45 people each night had responded to a salvation altar call, but there had been no "break" in the meetings.

On the third night the emcee had only permitted the congregation to sing one song, and then the choir had shared its musical contribution to the evening. Following their effort, the leader of the Assemblies of God for that region explained they had invited the speaker (me) to come from the other side of the world and they wanted to give him (me) plenty of time to speak. And he turned the service over to me.

With due respect to that wonderful man of God, the service was not ready. It actually seemed "deader" than the night before. As I was walking to the podium, I was sending an SOS heavenward. "What do I do with this meeting? It is not ready yet for the preaching of God's Word."

Instantly, I heard instructions from the Spirit of God about inviting the people to join me in a few moments of worship before I would preach. I began to share those instructions by observing the following;. "It takes two wings for a bird to fly.

5

And in the same way, it takes both the wing of worship and the wing of the preaching of God's Word for this bird called a service to fly." So, I invited them to lift their hands and hearts with me for a few minutes of worship.

After several minutes of this worship, which felt like forever to me, we experienced a "suddenly" from heaven. What my wife described as "a wind" blew down the steps that led from where she was sitting in the tent to the road above it. That wind became like a whirlwind blowing throughout the tent. After 30 or so minutes of this intense atmosphere, I felt led by the Spirit to give a salvation invitation. Somewhere between 400 and 600 people responded. I actually delayed my sermon until after that altar call. After a brief message on the manifest Presence of God, over 300 were baptized in the Holy Spirit. On the following night, I preached a full-length sermon, and somewhere between 600 and 900 people ran to the altar to repent of their sins.

It became a clear example of "both/and." We need the work of the Spirit, and we need the Word of Truth.

We must not see the move of the Spirit as something that is opposed to the preaching of God's Word. Both wings are necessary. This is not "either/or;" rather, it is a "both/and."

I need the wind of the Spirit to blow, but I also need the Word of God. I must be able to recognize seasons in revival. I need to be able to know when to open the Scripture and preach the Gospel. I also need to know the times when I should lay aside my prepared sermon and let the wind blow *"where it listeth"* (John 3:8 — KJV). Even as a preacher, I must admit I have seen times when a preacher was so insistent on preaching the sermon he had prepared, that he missed a timing of the Spirit. In some cases, he actually killed what God had in mind. I need to plead "guilty" to the above action myself.

As we were approaching the middle of the 1990s, many of our churches were probably pretty strong on Truth. Many sermons were well thought out. The content was excellent. However, many of us were not as comfortable with the moving of the Spirit.

6

As the winds of revival began to blow, I found myself reminding many of my colleagues that Jesus spoke of both *Spirit and Truth* (John 4:23 — KJV). I desperately need the Truth of God's Word. But I also need the activity of the Spirit. We had become strong on Truth and relatively weak on Spirit. I was being encouraged to simply "let the wind blow." And how the wind did blow!

The pendulum, though, has a tendency to go to the extremes. If some churches were strong on the Truth and weak on the Spirit preceding the '90's revivals, the opposite began to become true for some in the following years. In more recent years, I have felt required to suggest we needed both Spirit and Truth, with an emphasis on Truth. Some churches today have become very strong on the Spirit but weak on Truth.

Please hear my heart. I would campaign for both. We must not view church life as "either/or." We must see it as a "both/and."

There will be moments the Holy Spirit would like us to lay down the planned agenda. There are moments we need to "just let go, and let God." And there are also moments we need to clearly declare the Word of God. That Word may be a prophetic message. It may be a teaching that is long overdue. Straightforward evangelistic preaching will also be a necessity.

Dangers of Extremes in Revival?

Satan hates revival because he is well aware of the benefits it produces. His first strategy then is to keep revival from happening.

If he cannot do that, he will be glad to try to push revival off to an extreme — a place that is actually out of the flow of the river. If you have ever watched the flow of a river, you may notice that even while a strong current may be flowing in the middle of the stream, along the banks of the river may be places where it appears the current is not flowing. The middle of the stream may have clear water, while along the banks debris is evident. Satan will always seek to push your river of revival off course. He will seek to move you into a tangent of some sort.

7

History tells of a number of moves of the Spirit that ultimately went bad. The revival had a good start. Many wonderful things took place. Yet, the end of it was not good. Sometimes revivals have collapsed because of the moral failures of its leaders. Some revivals have prematurely ended because of excess. In some cases, poor theology has led to the demise of a revival.

While solid preaching may not eliminate the problems that can come with any move of God, I would suggest that solid Biblical preaching certainly reduces those issues.

What Does Revival Preaching Look Like?

In one sense revival preaching is just like any other type of preaching. However, in another sense revival preaching is totally different. If I may reference the '90s revival at the Brownsville Assembly of God, I would say it had a wonderful balance. Evangelist Steve Hill preached repentance all week, and then Pastor John Kilpatrick fed the church on Sunday. Wednesday through Saturday nights, the gospel net was cast and hundreds or even thousands of people found themselves at the altar turning away from sin and turning their lives to Jesus. Then, on Sunday morning Pastor Kilpatrick would open the Word of God and disciple those new converts as well as feed the seasoned saints in his church.

The similarities between Steve and John were evident. Both took a passage of Scripture as their starting point. Both sought to apply that passage to the audience to whom they were speaking. Both were gifted, anointed communicators. However, the focus when Steve preached was repentance toward our sin and faith in the Lord Jesus Christ. He was drawing the lost toward salvation. Pastor Kilpatrick would then open the Bible and explain how one lives for Jesus as a learner-follower of Him. The evangelist brought us to the Cross, and after the encounter at the Cross, the pastor taught us what it means to live after one has been to the Cross.

I noticed that when revivals broke out in the '90s, some pastors were tempted to repeat in the Sunday morning worship service what I was doing during the evening revival meetings. Certainly, we must always include the Gospel in our preaching, but preaching in revival is not the same as ministry to the family.

I believe revival preaching will emphasize the following: salvation (repentance for the sinner), sanctification (repentance for the saint), Holy Spirit, healing or faith, and the Presence of God.

I am capable of teaching seminars on a variety of subjects, but when I am preaching in revival as the evangelist or as a revivalist, my focus is fairly narrow. The above things become my focus. Indeed, during the greatest revivals in which I have been privileged to participate, salvation, sanctification, and/or Presence have made up the overwhelming majority of my preaching.

After five weeks of a move of God in a church where around 250 people had responded to a salvation-type of altar call, I was asked by the pastor if I could preach on a different topic. I gathered from the conversation that he was coming under pressure from his board regarding the content of the messages I was preaching. They wanted to know if I could preach on something else. I responded in the following manner. Was it possible for me to preach on something else? Yes, I have enough confidence in the Word of God, and probably enough ego, to believe that with 24 hours of study, I could preach on most topics from the Scripture. Would I preach on something else? The answer was, "No." I went on to say this: "We are in a season of harvest, and every farmer knows when the harvest is ready, you only have a short window to reap that harvest. As long as this harvest is happening, I will keep gleaning the harvest." If the season changed, I could preach on a variety of topics as the need required. If the pastor felt it was time to change the focus of the extended meetings, I would be glad to recommend preachers who were skilled and anointed in those areas, but I was constrained to go after the harvest. The leadership did opt to go in a different direction. Some years later that pastor fell in my arms weeping. Over and over he expressed his regrets. He was a good man. It was a great church, and I am sure the board members were good men. However, they failed to really grasp the relationship between harvest and revival. That revival God had sent only lasted a short time after we left. Indeed, a colleague, who preached there later, described it as the deadest place he had ever delivered a sermon.

Keeping the Main Thing, the Main Thing

The main thing for the evangelist in a revival is to be found in 1 Corinthians 15:1-8. The Scripture, as penned, by the Apostle Paul states, *"Moreover, brethren, I declare unto you the gospel which I preached unto you, which also ye have received, and wherein ye stand; By which also ye are saved, if ye keep in memory what I preached unto you, unless ye have believed in vain. For I delivered unto you first of all that which I also received, how that Christ died for our sins according to the scriptures; And that he was buried, and that he rose again the third day according to the scriptures: And that he was seen of Cephas, then of the twelve: After that, he was seen of above five hundred brethren at once; of whom the greater part remain unto this present, but some are fallen asleep. After that, he was seen of James; then of all the apostles. And last of all he was seen of me also, as of one born out of due time."* — KJV

In a message prepared to deliver to preaching evangelists, I observed the Holy Spirit, through the Apostle Paul, narrowed the focus of evangelistic preaching to three things:

THE DEATH OF JESUS;
THE BURIAL OF JESUS;
THE RESURRECTION OF JESUS.

Let me observe that you can conduct evangelistic events without being in revival. I have done them. For some years I participated in an outreach in the city of Chicago sponsored by the youth department of my state's denomination. It was great, but it was not revival. Every public meeting was focused on evangelism, and in some years a thousand people got saved in a few days. I loved it!

However, I would also observe that if you are in revival, evangelism will occur. Evangelism will feature evangelistic

10

preaching. Revival will include, but not be limited to, evangelistic preaching. In this section of this chapter, I will basically repeat the information I shared with those preaching evangelists. While revival preaching will involve more than evangelism, it is its core.

Evangelistic preaching will focus on Jesus. He must be exalted! Jesus is the message; the evangelist is just the messenger. It is important that we do not reverse those things. Neither the meeting nor the message is about me. The meeting is about the lost, and the message is about Jesus!

Evangelistic preaching will focus on who Jesus is, why He came to earth, what He did for humankind, and how Jesus can come into your life.

Evangelistic preaching reminds us that Jesus is the Son of God. He is more than a good teacher. He is more than a great philosopher. He is more than a compassionate philanthropist. He is the *"only begotten Son of God"* (John 3:16 – KJV). Jesus is uniquely different from any other being who has ever lived. He is both God and man!

He is the theme.

Our revival preaching will focus on His death. In a revival the evangelist must preach on sin. It was sin that nailed Jesus to the cross. It was my sin, and it was the sin of each member of the audience. Pulpit and pew are both culpable.

We must make it clear that sin will take sinners to hell. Sin has a very high price!

Years ago I heard a denominational executive say that you have to get them lost before you can get them saved. We must help people understand that unless Jesus is the Lord of their lives, they are not going to heaven. It is the realization that one is lost that often motivates them to be found.

I had been invited to preach in the great country of Germany. In a few days of preaching at a conference, over 90 people had responded to the repentance-based salvation message. We noticed our hostess, who spoke no English, was spending much time weeping. Our German was limited to two phrases, neither

11

of which was helpful, so we asked our interpreter if she could discover why our hostess seemed so distressed.

Apparently, when our hostess had gotten saved some years before, she did so because she was going through huge issues in her life. She was told Jesus would help her, and indeed He had. I believe she had gotten genuinely saved, but as I was preaching at that conference, the precariousness of her previous unsaved condition was becoming real. She had not just needed Jesus to help her through a difficult time, she had needed Him to deliver her from hell. The true penalty of sin was weighing in on her. Then, a burden for her unsaved friends was developed.

The preaching of the gospel in the atmosphere of revival brings the person face to face with the ugly reality of his sin and the terrible price it is going to exact on him.

Scripture reveals that the purpose of the law is to show us the helpless condition we are in. The proclamation of the gospel must include this component.

Too often we preach on sin in such a generic way that nobody knows what we are talking about. One of the great evangelists in New Zealand was famous for his "sin list." Somewhere during his preaching, he would go through a list of activities Scripture defined as sinful. I am sure some thought he was over the top with this list, but it did bring a practical reality to the message. If your activity was on the list, you knew you had sinned.

Not only must the evangelist preach on sin, but he or she must also preach on the blood. The shed blood of Jesus is the only remedy for sin. It is the required sacrifice that pays for my sin. That has never changed, and that will never change!

The preaching in revival will emphasize the Cross because that is the only remedy. Only the Cross can bridge the chasm between man's sin and God's holiness. Only the Cross can bridge the gap between man's guilt and God's justice.

Evangelistic preaching in revival will focus on His burial. We deal with historical realities, and then we make personal applications. Jesus died and was buried so that we could come out of our graves.

12

The Gospel is more than sentimentality. A real man was crucified on a real cross, and then His body was placed in a real tomb. In a very real way, His death and burial become mine. He took on Himself my sin. I was crucified with Christ. I was buried with Him.

Revival preaching will focus on His resurrection. This is a focus on His Deity. Yes, He was fully man, but He was and is fully God. Do I totally understand God becoming man? NO! It is beyond my pay grade, but I embrace it. I receive it.

The resurrection is a focus on hope. Do not leave the sinner hopelessly lost in hell. There is a remedy! The Gospel is not gloom and doom. It is more than hell-fire and brimstone.

Revival preaching confronts the sinner with the reality of his sin in the atmosphere of Holy Ghost conviction. But it also comforts him with the compassion of Christ.

A pastor of a church where revival had indeed broken out described the atmosphere in the following.: "I have never felt the conviction of the Holy Spirit and the compassion of Christ at that level." It was tangible in the atmosphere, but it was also an element of the preaching.

How you will deal with these cardinal truths will depend upon your target audience. Preaching to those who have never heard the Gospel is different from preaching to those who have the Bible memorized.

When I preached on the streets of Canar, Ecuador, the message I preached was very simple. The following is almost a verbatim quote of the message I proclaimed.

"There is a God in heaven. This God loves you and has a wonderful plan for your life. He wants you to come and live with Him in His home. However, there is something which will keep this wonderful plan of God from happening for you. That thing is called sin. Sin is disobeying God. It is doing something God has told you not to do. Or, it is not doing something God has asked you to do. Sin will keep you out of God's heaven. However, God loves you and sent His Son to take the punishment for your sin.

13

If you will believe Jesus is God's Son and ask Him to forgive you of your sin, He will come into your life today."

Most of the people I was preaching to had never heard the Gospel before. I was carrying the anointing from the Brownsville Revival, and scores of people came forward on the streets to give their lives to this Jesus.

When I preach in churches during an outpouring, I am dealing with a mix of people.

Steve Hill described four types of people in the Brownsville Revival. I have found the same. Some people are close to the truth. This type is represented by the Ethiopian eunuch in Acts 8. They are searching...they are not far from finding the truth.

Some people are distant from the truth. The Samaritan woman of John 4 represents this group. Her lifestyle was far removed from the truth. However, she was hungry for reality.

Luke 15 pictures a third group in the story of the prodigal son. These are those who have known the truth and have fallen away. These are the backsliders and those living with sin, both known and unknown, in their lives. Some backsliders are far away from the church, and some sit in its seats every week.

The final group of people is those who have already received the truth and are living in victory. This group is represented by Lydia in Acts 16.

Some of the above groups need a simple explanation of the nature of their spiritual condition just like the people of Canar, Ecuador, did. Some need to have their sin exposed. Some need to have their pride broken...critical spirit challenged... religion revealed.

The goal of gospel preaching in a revival is to bring people to a saving knowledge of Jesus. I am not just giving a speech. I am going to call people out of a life of sin and into a walk of obedience to the Word of God. That target affects everything in the preparation for the message. From start to finish, I am going after the harvest.

14

The passage in 1 Corinthians 15, quoted previously, deals with two additional aspects of this preaching. Notice how often the quoted verses use the phrase "according to the Scriptures." The authority for revival preaching is still the Scripture. This is especially true when the preacher is going after the harvest. The opinion of the sinner is just as valid as my opinion. However, the Word of God trumps both of our opinions. The great evangelist Billy Graham would often say, "The Bible says!" Fill your message with God's Word.

Notice, as well, the role of personal testimony. The passage mentions the story of Cephas, the twelve, 500 hundred brethren, James, all the apostles, and finally Paul himself. Steve Hill, from the Brownsville Revival, would share his own story. He was a drug addict. He had spent time in jail. Jesus rescued him. His personal testimony sealed the message. If Jesus did that for Steve, then perhaps Jesus will do that for me. You are not the message, but your audience needs to know the message works in your life as well.

The Preparation To Preach

As revival preachers, we are committed to the preaching of the Gospel. That is, we must believe in preaching. As an evangelist, I rejoice in every means and method of communicating the Gospel of the Lord Jesus Christ. However, I am still committed to the place preaching plays in the spread of the Gospel.

If I really believe in the efficacy of preaching, then I must make preparation to preach.

I relate to the words of the Apostle Paul in Romans 1:15 (KJV), "*So as much as is in me, I am ready to preach the gospel to you who are in Rome also*" (underlining mine).

The role of preaching is revealed by Jesus when He said in Mark 16:15 (KJV), ... "*Go ye into all the world and preach the gospel to every creature.*" This is the word He gave to His disciples at the end of His earthly ministry. At the beginning of it He had

15

said, *"The Spirit of the Lord is upon me, because he has anointed me to preach the gospel"* (Luke 4:18 — KJV).

But what does it mean to preach the gospel? If I count them correctly, there are four Hebrew words and five Greek words translated as *preach* in the King James Version of the Bible. They really boil down to two thoughts.

The Greek word *kerussw* (Kerusso — [kay-roos'-so]) appears approximately 61 times in the New Testament. It carries the thought of proclaiming with the suggestion of formality, gravity, and with an authority that must be listened to and obeyed. The focus then, is on the authority or the power of the message spoken on behalf of another. For example, a herald brings a message from the King, or an ambassador brings a message from his nation to another.

One of the Hebrew words occasionally translated as *preach*, but more often as *prophesy*, is *naba*, and it means "to be under the influence of the Divine Spirit." The authority for our preaching comes when we are under the influence of the Holy Spirit. Sometimes, this has been described as the Divine Unction.

The second main thought comes from the Greek word *euaggelizw* (euaggelizo — [yoo-ang-ghel-id'zo]). This word appears approximately 55 times in the New Testament, and it means "to bring good news." In the New Testament it is the good news of the coming of the Kingdom of God, of the salvation to be obtained, and of what relates to that salvation. The focus of euaggelizo is on the content.

Those two main Greek words will provide the framework for the next chapter of this book. My target is to be both practical and inspirational as I look at these two main issues…the content of evangelistic preaching and then the authority of evangelistic preaching in revival.

CHAPTER TWO

THE CONTENT OF EVANGELISTIC PREACHING

The goal of evangelistic preaching is to bring people to a saving faith in the Lord Jesus. I am not just giving a speech. As an evangelist I am not giving "a little talk." I am going to call people out of a life of sin and into a walk of obedience to the Lord, as revealed in the Word of God. That target affects everything I do in the preparation for the message. From start to finish, I am going after the harvest. We will deal with the altar call in another chapter, but let me say just this, I start the altar call when I start to preach.

Not only must I keep the main thing the main thing, I must also keep the main thing the plain thing. Evangelistic preaching needs to KISS (Keep It Simple Stupid). Try to avoid religious clichés that mean nothing to the sinner. During a revival service, I was inviting people to come to the altar, but a Catholic boy in the balcony could not figure out what the altar was in our Pentecostal church. Fortunately, someone recognized his plight and assisted him to the front of the building to receive prayer. I still invite people to the altar, but now I explain the altar is the front of the building.

I want to constantly examine my terms in preaching to be sure they are understandable to the one I am trying to reach. If I cannot avoid the cliché, then I explain what I mean by it. A number of years ago I was preaching in a Latin American country, and in the course of the message I made a reference to backsliders. I noticed the interpretation of that word seemed to go on a rather long time. Afterwards, the missionary explained

17

there was no one word in the Spanish language for *backslider*, so he had to explain to people they once were living for Jesus but had walked away from Him and were no longer living for Him. Now, when I use the term backsliders, I will go ahead and explain what I mean. By linking a definition with a religious term, I am both giving understanding to the uninformed of the meaning of my message, and I am also giving teaching to them for future reference.

Sometimes in evangelistic preaching, we may use a Biblical story as a reference, assuming everybody present knows and understands the story and its spiritual significance, but the sinner may not have a clue. My wife once sat in a Sunday school class in the inner city of Chicago with a young lady who had never heard of Jonah and the whale. The young lady was astounded to hear of a fish swallowing a man. I once witnessed to the sister of a university classmate who had never heard of Adam and Eve. Of course, our preaching must be from the Bible, but when you are preaching evangelistically, be sure your references are already understood or be prepared to give a simple explanation.

I preach often on David and the Ark of the Covenant, but the average sinner does not have a clue what the ark is. So, I will usually pause and explain that the Ark was, basically, the most sacred piece of furniture in the Old Testament worship and that it represented the Presence of God.

Evangelistic preaching not only needs to be simple, it needs to be clear and practical. The audience needs to know what you said. They need to know what they are to do about it. Clarity and practicality were among the strongest of my father's preaching gifts. He was fond of saying, "Put the candy on the lowest shelf so that the little lambs can reach it as well as the giraffes." Steve Hill, from the Brownsville revival, often said he was preaching for eight year olds! You are not preaching to impress people with your oratorical skill. You are seeking to make clear the Gospel with the intent of people getting saved.

Evangelistic preaching needs to be short enough that you do not lose the sinner and long enough to allow the Holy Spirit to intensify conviction. The longer you serve as an evangelistic preacher, the more you will discover this is a constant battle, for the longer you are in ministry, the more stories you know, and you will be tempted to tell them all!

Evangelistic preaching needs to know where it is going. Years ago I read a quote which is valid here, "Those who aim at nothing usually hit it." This speaks to actual sermon preparation.

Personal styles may vary even as personalities vary. My personal style follows.

I read a passage asking, "What does this passage say to me as I read it?", or "What did the Spirit impress upon me as I read it?" In line with this, "What does the passage mean within its original context?"

Next, I like to see what parallel and related passages say. Scripture does a wonderful job interpreting Scripture. If the passage from which I am preaching is in the Gospels, what do the other Gospels say about the event?

What do other translations say on this passage of Scripture? Sometimes a particular translation really brings a truth out. The balance of reading multiple translations may keep one from a bias expressed by a translator. This is particularly true of single author translations.

If time and resources permit, my next step in sermon preparation is to look into the key words in the passage from which I am preaching. A good concordance or a good Bible study program is helpful at this point. You can research the various shades of meaning of the key words in your passage.

I like to use commentaries and study Bibles as my checks and balances. After I am reasonably confident I have determined the meaning of a passage, I will look to see what the scholars of the past and present have to say about it. If my basic understanding is similar to what they have derived from the passage, I feel pretty safe to share it. However, if I am seeing something no one else is seeing, I should proceed with great caution. Indeed, if I realize I am totally different from other preachers I will re-examine what I am teaching. It may be that God has given me an insight that others have missed. That is not beyond the realm of possibilities. For example, I find often that the commentators of the past may not be helpful on things related to the move of the Spirit. Most scholars who wrote prior to 1900 will not have the same understanding of Acts 2 as those of us who live after 1900 have received. However, I must be aware if I am the only one seeing a particular "truth," I may simply be off and need to rethink my position.

Here is a simple three point formula for Biblical study you may find helpful:

1. What does it say?
2. What does it mean?
3. How does it apply to life today?

As I am preparing to preach, I will take notes on the material I am studying. Note-taking styles may vary from person to person. My personal style was taught to me by my journalism professor in a community college.

First, I create a preliminary outline (thesis/subject idea). From preliminary study I have an idea of what I feel I should share. From those thoughts I will create my preliminary or "working" outline.

Then I begin to take notes on the subject I am preaching. Those notes are assigned to a given point of the outline. I may do this as I move along in the note taking, or I may assign them to the outline after a period of note taking. In either case, I will come to a point where I review and edit. During this time I will examine my preliminary outline or thesis, then, evaluate the material I have researched. This helps me to know what needs to be made stronger and what has been covered adequately. Sometimes I have had to change the thesis because the material did not support it. In other words, either I was wrong in what I believed, or at least it cannot be supported from that passage of Scripture.

After time to review and edit, I will add additional notes to those areas that were weak. Then I rewrite my outline. Sometimes I may need to rewrite it several times. On other occasions the first draft was all that was necessary. I would like to think that was because I was hearing from God very clearly.

Perhaps at this point, I should pause and ask a question that should have been asked earlier. I remember as a young man, knowing God had called me to preach, going to my father, who was also my pastor, and asking him a question that made perfect sense to me. "Dad, how do I get a sermon?"

He responded by telling me to pray until God speaks to my heart. I thought surely there must be an easier way. However, I have found my father was basically right.

Let me share with you the five sources for sermons I use. Number one is that which Dad gave to me. I simply pray until I feel like I have heard the voice of the Lord.

Number two is the reading of God's Word. I do not read the Word of God to get a sermon, but often, what God speaks to me in my own reading for my own welfare will apply to others. As an evangelist you will find the Word of God has many ways of telling the Story. In fact, your gift of being an evangelist will cause you to read the Word of God from that perspective, and you will see evangelism...you will see the Gospel message in passages where others will not see it.

My third source is my sermon seed file. I keep a file with sermon ideas. In my situation I have a file in my computer. Prior to that, I had a file folder in my file cabinet. Your sermon seed file could be as simple as a box with scraps of paper in it. This sermon seed file is where I write down sermon ideas that come to me at various times. I jot down the idea, the verse of Scripture, the skeleton of an outline or whatever, then, place it in that file. When I am called upon to preach and no message is "hot," then I will go to this file to see if something I have written down and filed away may be the Word the Lord has for that moment. Some seeds may never germinate into a message.

Some may sit there for years, then, suddenly they sprout into a fruitful message.

My fourth source of sermons is the preaching of others. Someone once said to steal from one is plagiarism but to steal from many is research. Often when I hear another preacher preach, he or she may say something that will become the seed of a different message for me. It may be just one line or one thought. Rarely would it be the entire message. Some time ago I heard a friend preach on Joseph's coat of many colors. His emphasis was on the fact that it was the coat his father had given him, so Joseph wore the coat in spite of the opposition of his brothers. That whole idea stayed with me, and I ended up preaching an entire message from that concept.

Finally, events in life may be quickened by the Spirit. An evangelist will often use events in the news as a launching pad into the Gospel. The events of 9/11 that changed the world also prompted numerous salvation sermons. However, the event does not need to be of that size. Sometimes, a very simple event may be the spark for a salvation message. One time a simple greeting in a lunch line sparked a thought that I later turned into an effective message. Jesus frequently took events in life to drive home a message. For example, He used a withered tree to teach a lesson on faith to His disciples.

Once you know what you are preaching, you need to prepare your outline. You will need to find the approach that works best for you, and the approach that works best in your situation.

Some use no notes ever. They prefer to speak without any outline in front of them. If I am speaking in an evangelistic street meeting, I almost never use notes. Usually, this will mean the message is fairly simple.

Most evangelists will use some type of outline. My father's outlines consisted of key words which would bring a whole series of thoughts back to him. I normally preach from a sentence outline. In other words, most of my outlines are either sentences or phrases. As I am writing this material, I am basing it from a sentence outline I taught from at a conference for preaching evangelists.

One of my mentors preached from a complete manuscript. That is, he wrote out every word of his messages. During one period of my life, I had a five-minute radio broadcast four times per week. I always spoke from a manuscript for that program. The secret in manuscript preaching is to learn to speak it, not read it. To do this I would always be reading at least one sentence ahead of what I was speaking. So, I would be reading one thing and speaking another.

Others will memorize their material.

The main thing here is to know your material. Whatever method you use, become well-acquainted with the material you are preaching. The Holy Spirit may take me in a total different direction than I had planned, but normally, I know my material. Dr. James Brown suggests that to cement them in your mind, you read your notes (manuscript) over at least three times before going to the pulpit.[1] I have found that to be good counsel and normally try to practice that.

Tools of the Trade

Let us look at the "tools of the trade." I am going to suggest several tools to help you in your preparation of sermons. I recognize not all of these are going to be available to all of my readers. I can only suggest you use what is available to you at the moment. If your finances permit it at all, I encourage you to invest into these tools. A carpenter invests in quality tools to be able to do the job he is going to do. My dentist has invested in a number of "tools" to help him take care of my teeth. So the evangelist should invest in tools to help him/her preach more effectively to the lost.

Tool number one is so simple many overlook it. It is a good Bible. Some preachers have a Bible they read from and another one they preach from. The latter often being a large print version. I personally did not practice that approach. In fact, over the years I have tried to purchase a new Bible that was identical to my old so that all verses of Scripture were on the same place on the page (right hand page...left hand column... two thirds of the way down). More recently, I preach from my laptop computer or tablet and use their Bible programs for both reading and preaching.

The next tool, which is probably the most important, is some sort of Bible concordance. *Strong's Exhaustive Concordance* is probably the most well-known. It will have every word in the King James Bible listed, and it will also have the literal meaning of that word. It will also list every other way that Greek or Hebrew word is translated. *Young's Analytical Concordance* will group verses together by the actual Greek or Hebrew word. Concordances are now coming out for the NIV, as well. In many places Bible programs for computers are available and carry concordances on them. The program I am currently using contains *Strong's*, *Thayer's Greek-English Lexicon*, and *Brown-Driver-Briggs Hebrew and English Lexicon*. I have also found Bible resources available through various web sites.

The third tool I would recommend is a good word study book. *The Theological Wordbook of the Old Testament* and *Brown-Driver-Briggs Hebrew and English Lexicon* are good sources for the Old Testament. Either *Vine's Expository Dictionary of New Testament Words* or *Thayer's Greek-English Lexicon* are solid tools for the New Testament. Not to sound a well familiar refrain, but these are available on a good Bible program as well.

The fourth tool is a Bible dictionary. These are usually available on computer Bible programs. A Bible dictionary is often a cross between a dictionary and an encyclopedia.

Many have found a good topical study book such as *Nave's Topical Bible* to be an excellent tool. Once again, most computer Bible programs will have this feature.

Tool number six is commentaries. Commentaries can be devotional in nature or more analytical in focus. For the most serious student, the latter is probably more important, although the preacher will get benefit from both types. I have both types in my personal library. Some commentaries are whole Bible commentaries, while others focus on individual books. Probably the most well-known commentary on the whole Bible is *Matthew Henry's Commentary on the Whole Bible.* The strength of this type of commentary is it will provide you with material on nearly every passage of Scripture. Its weakness tends to be its inconsistency. In other words, it is hard for most authors to be equally proficient on every passage in God's Word.

Individual book commentaries may be very strong on a given book. However, to amass a strong library on every book is often almost, if not entirely, cost prohibitive. Another option is a set on the Bible written by different authors under the same editorial leadership. *The Pulpit Commentary, The Preacher's Homiletic Commentary, The Biblical Illustrator,* and *The New International Commentary* on the New Testament, and *The New International Commentary on the Old Testament* are examples of this. Even this does not totally escape the potential weaknesses of a commentary on the whole Bible. Any commentary will bring a theological bias with it. A commentary is not infallible. It is the studied opinion of a writer/scholar on the Word of God. As mentioned earlier, I usually use the commentaries as a checks and balances system in my own study of a passage.

I use a study Bible in the same way I use a commentary.

The seventh tool the preacher will find helpful relates to illustration sources. Illustrations are windows that permit the light to enter. They often can bring the truth of a message home to the hearer. Sources for illustrations are varied. Let me mention six. Even as I begin to mention these, I am aware the list is not complete. The Bible itself provides illustrative stories. The New Testament reveals one purpose of the Old Testament is to serve as an example for us living in the last days (1 Corinthians 10:11). Many are finding the internet to be a rich source of illustrative material. For those without access to the Internet, a number of books with topical illustrations are available in bookstores. For years I kept a file folder in my cabinet for illustrations. Today, I also keep one in my computer. That file can be as detailed as you wish. General reading is always a good source for illustrations. The evangelist can find illustrations in the newspapers and/or magazines he reads. Great works of literature can be sources of illustrations. Media (television/movies/radio/music) illustrations often resonate clearly with many in the general public. There is a lot of television, digital media, et cetera, that I would discourage one from watching but the facts are most of our audience does watch, and an occasional illustration from those sources not only communicates to some, but also suggests the evangelist is up to date with the real world. Speaking of real life, I often use real life or personal stories as illustrations. Evangelists tend to be storytellers. While that is not improper...and I am a storyteller...the evangelist needs to remember the story is usually not the message. Let the illustration illustrate, not dominate. Of course, social media has become a source of illustrations as well.

Finally, while many preachers read widely, others, such as Smith Wigglesworth, a great healing evangelist of the 1900s, read only the Bible. You will have to be persuaded in your own mind. If you have a Smith Wigglesworth type of ministry, you probably should not become too involved with other types of reading. However, most evangelists will probably find these tools to be important.

Keeping the Main Thing the Fun Thing

Speaking of illustrations, it is important to keep the main thing the fun thing. Make your preaching interesting. Never forget your content is central, but if you put them to sleep, then you have not helped them.

Illustrations and stories are windows to let the light in. Jesus was a storyteller, but a sermon must be more than an excuse to tell a story you want to tell. Evangelists have become infamous for having many stories but little Biblical substance to their preaching. I am a storyteller, but I work to keep the story in the role of servant, not master.

26

Steve Hill did very effective illustrated sermons. He probably preached at least one illustrated sermon a week during the life of the Brownsville (Pensacola) revival.

One illustrated sermon I have used (and I am sure others have done it as well) is called "Blind, Bind, and Grind." The basis is the story of Samson. I will blindfold a volunteer and talk about how sin blinds you. It blinds you to its existence, and it blinds you to its consequences. Then, I will tie up that volunteer and talk about how sin binds you. Sin will place the sinner in bondage. Finally, I will have the blindfolded, tied-up volunteer walk around an object. As they are doing this, I will talk about how Samson ended his life walking in a circle grinding grain. The focus here will be how sin destroys the sinner both in time and in eternity.

On a personal basis, I have found that preaching to kids and youth helps me communicate with adults. If I can keep the attention of the 8-or-9-year old, I will keep the adults as well. I always feel successful when a young student talks to me about what I was preaching.

As an evangelist I believe we should keep the main thing the current thing. Stay abreast of trends in culture, church, subgroups, et cetera.

Evaluate yourself for communication obstacles. How about listening to an audio CD or podcast or watching a DVD or YouTube® of yourself for the purpose of self-critiquing? I confess I cannot stand to watch myself preach, but I have adjusted to hearing myself. In listening I have noticed little things I had fallen into that were a hindrance to preaching. I personally do not use my wife as a sounding board or a critic for my preaching.

The Authority of Evangelistic Preaching

The authority of evangelistic preaching comes from the power of the Word of God—so preach the Word—1 Thessalonians 1:5 (KJV) says, "For our gospel did not come to you

27

in <u>word</u> only, but also in power, and in the Holy Spirit and in much assurance, as you know what kind of men we were among you for your sake."

Tim LaHaye, well known preacher and author, quotes an elderly preacher as saying, "Give them the beefsteak of the Word of God and the spice of your personality."[2] Some preachers reverse that instruction. When they preach, you see the beefsteak of their personality and a little spice of the Word of God.

I have read where Billy Graham noticed the difference once he settled in his mind the authority of the Word.

Our Lord Himself taught us by example that you overcome the devil with the Word of God. When Satan came to tempt Him, He responded with, "It is written."

God has built an authority into His Word that goes to the heart of the sinner, so use the Word. Some evangelists spend too much time defending the Sword of the Spirit, when we would be better off just to use it. The Word of God carries power. I have been amazed at how the simplest preaching of Scripture brought great conviction. On one occasion I was preaching in Argentina. I preached a message from the familiar Roman road of salvation. After watching four teens get saved, the missionary's wife said she had never heard a more simple and plain declaration of the Gospel. The fruit came because of the power of the Word not the eloquence of the evangelist. This does not suggest preaching is simply stringing verses of Scripture together. It is to say. "Keep your evangelistic preaching full of the Word of God."

Not only does the authority of revival preaching come from the Word of God, it also comes from the anointing of the Holy Spirit. So seek to preach the Word of God in the power of the Spirit. Observe again 1 Thessalonians 1:5 *For our gospel did not come to you in word only, but also in power, and in <u>the Holy Spirit</u> and in much assurance, as you know what kind of men we were among you for your sake.*

It is the anointing of the Holy Spirit that lifts a sermon from simply being a speech and causing it to become life-giving truth and reality. We read in 2 Corinthians 3:6 (KJV), *"Who also made us sufficient as ministers of the new covenant, not of the letter but of the Spirit; for the letter kills, but the Spirit gives life."* The anointing (sometimes called the unction) brings the "that's it" to preaching. The anointing takes the Word of God and drives it home to the heart. The anointing causes the Word to become an arrow of the Lord striking the target of the human heart. On more than one occasion after hearing a strongly-anointed evangelistic message, a listener has told me they felt like an arrow had hit their heart.

I pray Psalm 51:11 every day, *"take not away thy Holy Spirit"* (KJV). This emphasis on the anointing is so simple, but I do not think I can state it too strongly. Style may impress people but anointing changes them. I am totally dependent upon the anointing. I seek to be as simple and direct as I can be in evangelistic preaching, and then trust the Holy Spirit to drive the truth to the hearts. The yoke is still *"destroyed because of the anointing"* (Isaiah 10:27 – KJV).

I was impressed as a young preacher by a statement Yongi Cho made regarding the Holy Spirit. He said he usually left the seat next to him empty. He called it the seat of the Holy Spirit. Before preaching he would lean over and say to the Holy Spirit, "Come, it is time for us to preach." Afterwards, he would always say, "Holy Spirit you did a good job."[3] During my years of pastoring, where I could control seating arrangements, I did the same thing. Of course, I knew the Holy Spirit did not need a seat. He lives in me, but it was an illustration to remind me of my total dependence upon Him.

During a message I was preaching in the Philippines, I noticed my interpreter was overcome with weeping while he was attempting to interpret the message. He explained what he was experiencing after the service. He served the Filipino church as an evangelist. While I was preaching and he was interpreting, the Lord began asking him if he was noticing the difference in what happened when he preached and what was happening while I was preaching. The Lord told him his preaching was full of hype and emotion, but this message was changing the life of the people who were listening. May I suggest, it is the powerful anointing of the Spirit that creates this. Indeed, while I was preaching that sermon, people began pouring into the altar before I could even give an altar call.

The third source of authority for revival preaching comes from the personal character of the revivalist. Notice again 1 Thessalonians 1:5, *"For our gospel did not come to you in word only, but also in power, and in the Holy Spirit and in much assurance, as you know what kind of men we were among you for your sake."* This same theme comes through in Acts 20:20 (KJV) where the Apostle says, *"I have showed you, and taught you."* As you read 1 Thessalonians chapter two, you will notice how Paul conducted himself among those he ministered to.

Who you are is every bit as important as what you say, in fact, possibly more so. Actually, that is understated. Some evangelists have short careers because they are offensive. There is a difference in the Word of God offending and me being offensive. I do not want to be offensive, even as I realize the Word of God will bring offense. So, I will work not to do things that are offensive personally, but I will never apologize for the Word of God offending some.

Some things are caught as much as they are taught. Your attitude, that is, your spirit, communicates. Some evangelists can preach about hell and make it sound like they are glad you are going while others will preach about hell with a broken heart for those who are going. It may sound like a cliché but people do not care how much you know until they know how much you care. I have seen people whom I had made angry come frequently and repeatedly to meetings; they kept coming back partially because they knew I cared.

Evangelistic preaching can become an event. People can be preached to but not at. You can only preach at people for a short time, but you can preach to people almost forever. You can only skin a sheep once, but you can shear them often. As an evangelist you need to know when to use "I" messages and when to use "you" messages. In an "I" message, you identify yourself with them. For example, instead of saying "you people need to come to Jesus," it is better to say "as people, we need to come to Jesus." This approach usually is better received and is more effective. A "you" message is confrontational and can become combative. I tend to switch from the "I" message to the "you" message during the conclusion and the altar call.

The authority of revival preaching comes from the signs and wonders of the Gospel, for in 1 Thessalonians 1:5, *For our gospel did not come to you in word only, but also in power...* Paul did not preach an empty gospel. Signs and wonders accompanied the preaching of the Word. Mark's Gospel records, *"And they went out and preached everywhere, the Lord working with them and confirming the word through accompanying signs."* (Mk 16:20 – KJV). These confirming signs and wonders may be powerful healings. Do we dare believe God to do these things as signs to the unbelievers? Recent reading has reminded me that significant healings have been a part of the Argentine revival. The signs and wonders may include the gifts of the Spirit. The Holy Spirit may share a Word of Knowledge (revelation of sin or a life situation). The heart is smitten by the confirming work of the Spirit.

The authority for evangelistic preaching comes from the assurance of the preacher. I quote 1 Thessalonians 1:5 again, *our gospel did not come to you in word only, but...in much assurance.* Are you convinced of your message? It you do not believe it, nobody else will, either. It must consume you before it moves others. Passion has a role to play, but it must not be play acting. Some preachers can make their truth sound like fiction, while some actors can make their fiction look like truth. Do you really believe your audience needs Jesus? Can you believe they are going to come to Him? To use a baseball analogy, you will not always hit a home run when you preach, but if you hit enough singles you will score runs as well. Keep the altar in front of the people. As you preach, build toward the altar.

A part of this assurance comes from knowing your audience. The message needs to fit the audience. For me to speak to grandmothers on how to raise their children may not be appropriate. You learn about your audience in at least three ways. First, ask questions. If you are speaking at an evangelistic event, ask your host some questions. Who is he expecting to come? Are you preaching to a church audience or to a largely unsaved audience? Are you preaching on the street or in a church building? Different rules apply in different places.

The second way you learn is to gain insight of the Holy Spirit. I pray for insight. I am also open to His insight even when I greet people before a meeting. On many occasions as I shake hands with someone before a meeting, the Holy Spirit will make me aware of their basic spiritual condition. This is called discerning of spirits. Often, I will know whom the unsaved are before I start to preach.

The third way I learn about the audience is to observe it during the early part of the service. I like to watch and pray. I always enter into worship personally, but I also attempt to monitor the crowd. You can learn much by simple observation. Do they know the songs? Are they restless? The more you know the group to whom you are preaching, the greater your assurance will normally be.

There is no greater privilege in the world than to be able to address men and women on behalf of God. As evangelists we are given the ministry of reconciliation (2 Corinthians 5:18). What a joy to tell others they can be reconciled to God! What a joy to tell others they can be made the righteousness of God through Jesus Christ!.

My preacher father was fond of saying, "A sharp ax cuts better than a dull one." As preachers of the gospel, we want our preaching to be the most effective we can make it to be. Develop your ability to make the content more effective. As someone complained about G. Campbell Morgan, "This man evidently has no use for language other than that of making people know what he wanted to say."[4] May that be said about you and your preaching! You will have to work to keep the ax sharp. However, you not only need a sharp ax, you also need a source of power to get the ax moving. *Euagellion* and *kerusso* are both needed. You need content and power.

Footnotes:
  [1] The source for this quote was an audio tape of James Brown, who was at the time the President of the Assemblies of God Theological Seminary in Springfield, Missouri.
  [2] *How to Study the Bible For Yourself* authored by Tim LaHaye and published by Regal Books.
  [3] The source for this quote was in a message I heard Yongi Cho preach. At that time he was the Pastor of the world's largest church in Seoul, South Korea.
  [4] G. Campbell Morgan in a little book titled *Preaching*.

CHAPTER THREE

BRINGING IN THE NET

The Preparation for the Altar

The altar call should be the highlight of the revival meeting. It is often the focal point of all that has been taking place. Yet for many preachers, the altar call is something with which they struggle. For many years in my own preaching ministry, the invitation was the weakest part of the message.

Let me suggest that preparation is essential for a successful altar call.

There is, first of all, personal preparation. Much of the preparation begins in my heart before any service happens. Let me ask you a question that I ask myself. What are you preaching for? What is the purpose of your preaching? Do you have a well-defined aim? Do you have a target? It has been well said, "Those who aim at nothing, hit it!"

What is the direction of the message? Can I identify in a short statement the purpose of the message? If I had to reduce my sermon to one statement, what would that statement be? Am I going after souls? Certainly, some public ministry in a revival is of a teaching variety, but often, revival preaching calls for action. Do I know what I believe the Holy Spirit wants to accomplish through the message?

It is my conviction the altar time is the response time. This is the time the hearer responds to what the Spirit has been saying to them. Don't allow them to leave without an opportunity to respond to that which God is speaking to them. Usually, people need someone to give them an opportunity to respond. Some time ago I was preaching a revival meeting in the States. When I gave the invitation on this Sunday morning, a backslidden pastor came from the balcony to recommit his life to Jesus Christ. In later conversation he told me he had been visiting services for months waiting for someone to give an altar call where he could get things right with God. Certainly, that decision could have been made at home. Certainly, he knew what he needed to do, and yet he still found he needed someone to actually call him to account and to give him the opportunity to say yes to the voice of the Spirit.

Often, when the invitation is not given at the close of the message, the sense of urgency felt by the hearer begins to dissipate upon returning home. I might argue this should not be so. Certainly, history is full of those who found conviction continued to grip them after fleeing a meeting. Yet quite often, the devil tries to steal conviction from the sinner. I suggest the best time to draw in the spiritual net is when the conviction of the Spirit is at work.

Let me urge you to begin to view the altar as your friend. It is the time to meet with God. It is the time to deal with the things the Holy Spirit has spoken to you about during a message.

In preparing for the altar, understanding the point or thrust of the message determines the primary point of the altar. Let me illustrate.

Preacher, have you ever given an altar call for non-tithers to start tithing? How about an altar call for non-givers to missions to start giving to missions? Or what about an altar call for people who were not praying daily to commit themselves to a certain amount of time in prayer daily?

I have given altar calls for all of the above. If the Holy Spirit gave me the message, then somebody in the audience needs it and needs to respond to it.

Furthermore, any message can be converted into a salvation call. Let's say I have been speaking on family and the necessity of the father assuming the role of the spiritual priest in his family. I might say something like this, "Sir, before you can be a spiritual priest in your family, you must first of all have a relationship with Jesus yourself. You cannot lead your family where you have not been. I am going to give you, and every man in this auditorium, an opportunity to make that decision to live personally for Jesus. I am going to ask now that every man who is not saved, and you know you need to be saved before being a spiritual leader in your family, to lift your hand right now" (or stand to their feet, or come to the front).

Perhaps, I have been speaking on healing. I might say something like this, "As wonderful as physical healing is, there is another type of healing that many in this place need. It is a healing for the sickness in your soul called sin. I would like to pray for every person," etc.

One of the best things I began doing as a Pastor was writing out my altar call. I give as much time to prepare for the altar call as I do any other part of the message. I believe the Holy Spirit can lead me in that preparation. Certainly, He can change it at the altar, but I find if I have prepared, then the altar is likely to be more effective. I try to think the altar call through. What do I want them to feel? What do I want them to think? What do I want them to do?

Let me stress something here. DO NOT HURRY THE ALTAR CALL—GIVE THE HOLY SPIRIT TIME TO WORK ON THE PERSON.

Not only do you need to prepare yourself, but you also need to prepare the congregation for the altar call. As an evangelist preaching an evangelistic message, the whole sermon is an altar call. At one time I was afraid of letting people know the invitation was coming. I was afraid the devil would put up their defenses, so I tried to sneak up on them.

But I have learned if I start the altar call when I start preaching, I am allowing the Holy Spirit time to deal with the sinner throughout the message. The sinner also has time to be thinking about it, so the decision is not rushed. Throughout the message I may say something like this, "In a few minutes I am going to ask you...and every person in this room who has not given their life to Jesus...to do so."

Finally, when you give an altar call, make the altar call clear! Do they know why they are coming to the front? Don't announce one call, and then surprise them at the front with something else. When you make the altar clear and honest, the Holy Spirit will do His office work.

Prepare yourself to give the invitation...prepare your congregation to respond to the invitation...and then give it.

Now, we will begin looking at the actual giving of the altar call.

Is Your Net Prepared?

I want to give credit for much of the material in this section to Evangelist Steve Hill. From 1996 until 2000, I probably heard Steve Hill, who served as the evangelist God used for the revival at the Brownsville Assembly of God where hundreds of thousands of people responded to a salvation invitation, give 75-100 salvation altar calls. That number is conservative.

Steve shared some great insights into preparing the net used for bringing souls into the Kingdom of God. These insights can be listed in a simple four point outline. First, prepare the net;, second, cast the net,; third, draw in the net; and fourth, repair the net.

A good fisherman keeps the net prepared. We are fishing for the greatest catch of all. Remember, Jesus called us to be fishers of men.

The preparation of the net begins from the beginning of the service. Be prepared to give the altar call from the beginning of your message. Basically, Steve Hill simply gave long altar calls. From the time he stepped into the pulpit until the close of his message, he was always preparing the people to respond to the invitation, to turn from sin, and to receive God's forgiveness. If you have ever listened to Billy Graham preach, you will note he did the same thing. From early in the message, he started preparing the net.

These giants of soul winning may say something like this, "In a few minutes…at the close of this message…I am going to give you an invitation to commit your lives to Jesus." Or they may say, "At the close of this message when I give an invitation for people to invite Christ into their lives, I want to encourage you to be a part of that number."

As a part of preparing the net, you need to know where you are going. You need to know your message. You need to know the heart of the Father for that meeting. You need to know how you plan on approaching the altar. Certainly, the Holy Spirit may give you spontaneous direction at the close, but by and large, that spontaneity is based upon much preparation of heart and mind.

Before throwing out the net have it ready. By this Steve Hill would seek to prepare the hearts of different groups of people in the meeting. He would seek to address every group or type of person he knew was in the meeting. For example, he would specifically speak to those who have never been saved. He would also speak to those who are backslidden. That is, he would talk to those who had once lived for the Lord but now were no longer living for Him, or to those who were now walking away from Jesus. At some point he would speak to those who were religious, but who were not intimate with the Lord. Finally, he would say something to those who had sin in their lives. He was very simple and very clear when speaking to them. He might simply say, "This invitation is for those who are doing things Jesus would never do." Most sinners seem to know they are doing things Jesus would never do.

Once he had prepared the net, then he would cast the net. First of all, make the invitation clear. Some altar calls I have heard are so obscure one could never be sure to whom the invitation was being given. Every person under the sound of your voice needs to know exactly whom you are calling to respond to the Lord.

I gave an invitation one Sunday in the States to a service of about 135 people. When I gave the salvation invitation, roughly

35-40 people responded, including half of the board of deacons. After the meeting the pastor was asking if I thought the people really understood the altar call. Before I could answer, his wife spoke up. Her comment was this, "They understood, it was very, very clear, and I have been praying for this." How delighted I was to know the invitation had not been cloudy!

In casting the net, do not shut the door on people by the way you are giving an invitation. Sometimes we are so concerned we might be offensive, we make people feel like the sermon really did not apply to them, anyway. Sometimes we let people off the hook too easily. We make it easy for people to not respond to Jesus. How often have I heard a preacher apologetically suggest nobody here really wants to get saved. I have heard some say, "if anyone here wants to get saved." Don't apologize for giving an invitation! You are giving to your listener the greatest invitation in the world! Make the net wide enough so every sinner can get saved. If by some chance a saint accidentally wanders into the net, the Lord is not going to punish you. While I never aim to bring condemnation, I am learning to let the Holy Spirit bring conviction. Don't preach a great sermon, and then allow them to walk away too easily.

After you have cast the net out there and they know to whom you are speaking, then draw the net in. Explain to them what you want them to do. Never assume sinners understand what they are to do. Sinners will not know how to get saved unless we walk them through the process.

When you give the invitation, explain exactly what you want them to do. I may say something like this,. "In just a moment the musicians are going to be singing a song. As they sing that song I want you to leave your seat. I want you to come to the front of this building. When you come to the front of this building, I want you to stand here facing me,"...or I may say, "I want you to kneel in front of this stage." If I tell them I want them to come to the altar, I will always explain what the altar is. I am remembering, again, the Catholic boy who wanted to commit his life to Jesus but saw nothing in that Pentecostal church that looked like the altar in the church he grew up attending. Leave nothing to chance.

When I draw in the net, I want the necessity of repentance to sink in. By coming to the front of this building, you are saying you want to turn away from sin. By coming to the front of this building you are turning toward God. Walk them through the process of what they are going to do and what God is going to do. When you come to the front of this building, I am going to pray with you. In that prayer we are going to ask the Lord to forgive us of sin and come into our lives. When you pray that prayer, the Lord is going to forgive you of your sin and come into your life.

Finally, Steve Hill would talk about repairing the net. Fix the holes in your net. You probably missed somebody the first time. There is probably someone in the meeting who would like to commit their lives to Jesus but is really struggling with the process. This is why I will often do what he did and have people turn to the person next to them and ask, "Should you be at the altar?" I may use some statement that reflects the heart of the message. For example, one time I spoke on getting in the wheelbarrow with Jesus. I actually had a wheelbarrow brought into the auditorium that I pushed around during the message. At the altar I asked the people to ask the person next to them if they needed to get in the wheelbarrow with Jesus?

Finally, make sure you are at peace in your heart before you close the altar. Yes, I wrestle with my comfort zone. Yes, I battle the fear of looking like a failure. Preacher, you are simply the messenger. You give opportunities; the Holy Spirit does the rest. One Sunday morning in Canada, the peace would not come until after the eighth invitation. On that invitation the Pastor's wife responded. Her personal testimony to me after the meeting confirmed it was a genuine salvation experience. Throw out the net!

CHAPTER FOUR

A PERSONAL REFLECTION ON
FIVE-FOLD MINISTRY IN REVIVAL

After visiting the Brownsville Revival in 1996, we entered the greatest season of our lives and ministry. In the following four years, two out of three meetings we were scheduled to preach turned into some level of revival.

Let me pause at this point to address a challenge I face in writing on revival. I acknowledge revival is larger than a series of meetings. The annual spring or fall series of meetings conducted by many churches is not revival. They are a series of meetings.

To be sure, it is entirely possible for revival to break out in one of those meetings. And often I have been privileged to be the preacher when that happened. But I also am aware revival itself may occur in a church without a series of special meetings being conducted.

Yet, often God uses evangelists as a primary carrier of His Word during the public meetings in revival. This is because the nature of the ministry of the evangelist is quite compatible with, I should say "vital to," revival. By that I mean that often the evangelistic preaching that occurred during those meetings was the heart of God that is a part of revival. That is not to lessen the value of any other ministry gift. Let me illustrate that.

A friend of mine, who traveled for years as a teacher with a strong emphasis on prayer, made the observation to me one day that it was not likely "revival" would break out in a church while he was at that church speaking. However, if the church

43

actually heeded and practiced the message he was bringing, revival would probably come.

Another pastor said to me,. "Revival is not likely to break out in direct response to my ministry, so I will need someone like you who is more likely to be the spark God will use to ignite the revival. However, for revival to sustain, it will need someone like me to nurture and disciple it."

May I say BINGO!

They have it down correctly. Every ministry gifting is needed in the flow of revival. We will still need the teacher to teach, the prophet to prophesy, and the pastor to counsel and comfort. We will still the apostle to connect the dots and give wise leadership to the whole.

But, it is highly likely the preaching ministry of the evangelist, at least in the early days, may receive more emphasis.

In 2010 my wife and I were the speakers for a 3-day meeting at Cross Tabernacle in Terre Haute, IN. Those three days turned into an ongoing, life-changing revival that continues, at this writing, eleven years after it started. Somewhere around the two-to-three-year mark, I remarked to the pastor (apostle) of that church that I sensed a change was coming.

I told him I was not going to call what I was going to say a prophetic word, although in hindsight it probably was. I told him that I believed God was going to begin to add more voices to the preaching of the revival as He sought to mature it. The voice of the evangelist had been the primary voice, but God was going to add more voices. The other gifts would increase. My voice would begin to diminish, as God added other voices. That did not mean my voice or ministry was not important, but that God would add voices representing other essential giftings. This is exactly what God did.

SECTION TWO

SERMONS I HAVE PREACHED DURING REVIVAL

In this chapter, the first that will deal with samples of revival preaching, I am going to share a message I preached frequently on Sunday mornings. In this message I attempt to bridge the role of the revivalist/prophet and the role of the evangelist. I attempt to stir up hunger for revival, explain what brings revival, and specifically call people to repentance and salvation.

CHAPTER FIVE

MAKING A PLACE FOR GOD

The text for this message is found in Exodus 25:8 (KJV), *"And let them make me a sanctuary; that I may dwell among them. According to all that I shew thee, after the pattern of the tabernacle, and the pattern of all the instruments thereof, even so shall ye make it."*

Some believe that if there is a God, then He created the universe and wandered off to the far side of it because He certainly is not interested in people (especially them). But, I want you to see God has always been very interested in people.

We read in Genesis 3:8 *"that they heard the voice of the Lord God walking in the garden in the cool of the day"* (KJV).

The impression is that each and every evening God came to spend time with Adam and Eve.

Can you imagine that?

Every day between the evening meal and bedtime the Lord God came to spend time with Adam and Eve. They would walk and talk in the garden. In the canvas of my imagination, I can see the Lord walking with Eve.

"Eve, do you see this flower? I made it for you."

47

Hey, there was nobody else there but Adam and Eve.

This wonderful relationship continued for an unknown period of time. In fact, it continued until sin destroyed the fellowship.

May I remind us that sin always destroys a relationship with the Lord. We also read in Genesis 3:8 that when *"they heard the voice of the Lord God...Adam and his wife hid themselves from the presence of the Lord amongst the trees of the garden"* (KJV). You see, sin had made Adam and Eve uncomfortable in the presence of God. Sin will always destroy your relationship with the Lord.

Let me demonstrate that. Do you remember as a child doing something you knew your parents did not want you to do... and then how uncomfortable you were because you were afraid they were going to discover what you did?

Have you ever told a lie about someone and then you were required to spend time with them...and you were not comfortable being around them because you did not know how much they knew of what you had said? When you sin against God, you cause something to come into the relationship that will sever that relationship.

Perhaps at this point we should define what sin actually is.

Sin is a violation of God's Word...of His laws...it is doing something that hurts and offends God. Sin is not sin because a church committee decided it is sin. Sin is not sin because a bunch of preachers got together and said, "Let's come up with a list of things we can command people not to do."

No, a thousand times, no! Sin is sin because it is something that is offensive to God. It is something that causes God to feel pain. Theologians, those are the really smart dudes, describe sin as coming in two packages.

The first package is what they call the sin of commission. It is called commission because it is something you committed. The sin of commission is doing something God has told you not to do.

We see this illustrated in Genesis 2:17. In Genesis 2:17 God had instructed Adam not to eat from one tree in the garden. May

I point out God was not being stingy. This was an entire garden. God only asked them not to eat from the fruit from one tree. They were free to eat the fruit from every other tree in that garden.

When Adam and Eve ate that fruit, they knowingly and willingly did something God had told them not to do. I emphasize this action on their part was "knowingly" and "willingly." They knew that what they were doing was something God had commanded them not to do, and nobody forced them to eat the fruit. Temptation comes to all of us, but we are the ones who make the decision to say yes to it.

1 John 3:4 says, *"Whosoever committeth sin transgresseth also the law: for sin is the transgresssion of the law"* (KJV). The NIV puts it in these words — *"Everyone who sins breaks the law; in fact, sin is lawlessness."* How many stop signs do I have to run before I am a law breaker? One…five…ten?

How many of God's laws do I have to break before I am a law breaker in the eyes of God?

Someone observed that the Ten Commandments were not ten suggestions.

God really does feel strongly about the things He said in His Word. They really are important to Him. When I do something God has said, "I don't want you to do that," I have sinned against Him. Period. Exclamation Point!

When I tell a lie, I have sinned. When I take something that belongs to someone else, I have sinned. When I have sex with someone I am not married to, I have sinned. When I say something about someone else that is not true, I have sinned.

But there is another term the theologians use. This second term is the "sin of omission." This is failing to do what I know I should do. James 4:17 (KJV) puts it in these words, *"Therefore to him that knoweth to do good, and doeth it not, to him it is sin."* Our relationship with people is not affected only by what we do. It is also affected by what we do not do.

When I was a boy and my mother was going shopping, she would leave us with a set of instructions we were to carry out while she was gone. Often this included doing the dishes and cleaning up our bedrooms. If I did the dishes but failed to clean up my bedroom, my mother seemed to feel I had not obeyed her. What I did not do was just as important as what I did. When I fail do that which I know I should do, I have sinned against God.

This sin of Adam and Eve did not change God's feelings and desires to have a people He could be in relationship with, but the sin had broken that relationship.

Christianity is actually the story of God trying to make it possible for Him and people to once again have this wonderful, intimate fellowship. I will have two simple points in this message – and then I want to give us opportunity to respond to God.

In our first point, I want you to see how much God desires to be in relationship with you. Second, I want you to see what is going to be required for you to be in that relationship.

God Desires To Be In a Relationship With You

Let's begin by seeing how much God desires to be in relationship with you.

Notice what God wants to do in Exodus 25:8, *"that I may dwell among them."* God says, "I want to dwell among them." For those interested in this sort of detail, the Hebrew word for *dwell* appears 129 times in the OT and the KJV uses the word *dwell* 92 of those times.

Strong's Concordance says, it carries "the idea of lodging; to reside or permanently stay. It can be used literally or figuratively." God is saying, "Fix me up a place because I want to come and live with you."

In the Old Testament, they built a physical place where God could come and live among them. Here in Exodus they made a tent for God. Solomon built a permanent structure for Him. However, the Old Testament was not the final revelation. It was the type and shadow as described with these words in Hebrews 8:5 (KJV), *"Who serve unto the example and shadow of heavenly things, as Moses was admonished of God when he was about to make the tabernacle: for, see, saith he, that thou make all things according to the pattern shewed to thee in the mount."*

That Old Testament tabernacle had been built according to the instructions given by God, but in the New Testament, the place of God's residence changes.

Hebrews 8:10 (KJV) reads, *"For this is the covenant that I will make with the house of Israel after those days, saith the Lord; I will put my laws into their mind, and write them in their hearts: and I will be to them a God, and they shall be to me a people:"*

God wants to move from a building to our hearts and minds. As a small boy, I would sing this song in church:

> *Into my heart, into my heart, come*
> *into my heart Lord Jesus, come in today,*
> *come in to stay, come into my*
> *heart Lord Jesus.*

We meet today in a place, a building, we have set aside for worship, but we understand the real place He wants to inhabit is our hearts and lives. At the close of this chapter, I want to give an opportunity for you to make room for Him in your heart and life.

Although the spirit of man is the dwelling place God desires, we find that God still delights in making His Presence known among us corporately. Have you ever been in a service where you felt an unseen Presence? You would say, " Wasn't the Presence of God wonderful…awesome…scary today?"

Historically, revival has been one of those seasons where God seems to make His presence a tangible, felt experience. In the revival in the Hebrides Islands, off the coasts of Scotland nearly two generations ago, a man came to a Pastor saying he had to get right with God. When the pastor said, "But I have not seen you in the meetings," the man said, "I have not been in the meetings, but this revival is in the air and I cannot escape it."

It was this manifest Presence of God that would often accompany the ministry of Charles Finney. Entire cities would seem to come under a blanket of God's Presence. It is this tangible Presence of God that has often been the earmark of extended services we have been involved with.

What God Requires For That Relationship

Secondly, I want you to see what is going to be required for you to be in that relationship. *"Let them make me a sanctuary."* Please notice they did the construction. Only you can make room for God in your life. I cannot get saved for you…I cannot surrender your life to Jesus.

Here are three things you must understand about this decision. First, you must make it personally. Your Pastors, no matter how godly they are, cannot build your personal dwelling place for Jesus. Young person, your mom and dad cannot make this decision for you. It is a personal decision.

Second, you must make this decision promptly. The Word of God says, *"behold, now is the accepted time; behold now is the day of salvation"* (2 Corinthians 6:2—KJV). You do not have a guarantee of tomorrow. This is the only day you are assured of having, so it is important you make this decision today. Make it promptly. Delay is dangerous.

And then third, you must make this decision perpetually. While salvation itself should be a forever, one-time decision, you do decide each day that you are going to make room for Jesus in that day. You will provide a place for Him in your life…heart…home…family…business. Will you make a place for Jesus today?

Church, only you can make the decision whether or not you will make a corporate sanctuary for Him. When I was pastoring my first church, I had a guest speaker who had spoken at the largest gatherings in the Assemblies of God. He asked me a great question, "Do you want revival, or do you want a few good services, because you can have either one?"

God can come and visit us from time to time, and that is wonderful, or God can come and dwell among us. But for the latter we have to prepare a place for Him. I would like to attempt to make you thirsty for Him. Matthew 5:6 promises, *"Blessed are they which do hunger and thirst after righteousness: for they shall be filled"* (KJV).

We were preaching what became a fifteen-week meeting in Michigan City, Indiana. One evening I was a bit late in arriving in the auditorium for the pre-service prayer meeting. Others were already praying when I hit the room speaking in tongues. I had gone roughly two-thirds of the way around the auditorium when it dawned on me something was different this night. I stopped my wife to ask, "Is it just me or is there something in this room tonight?" She asked me what I meant. I responded, "It is different. It is heavy in this room tonight." She asked me, "Is it bad?" I said, "No, it is wonderful. I feel like someone has just dumped honey all over me." She said, "Well, it is not you because I feel that, too." I had barely taken half a dozen steps when I heard the pastor say to his wife, "Sherry, is it just me…" It seemed from that night there was an increased Presence that had chosen to dwell with us. And it basically remained for the next year at that church.

Two years later I was preaching in a church in Paducah, Kentucky. The Lord spoke to the church through a prophetic word, "I have chosen to dwell in this place." During the run of those meetings, one to two hours of worship felt like only twenty minutes. Many nights I could do little more than lay on the floor on my face because of the thick Presence of God. During the altar time, I would often find myself praying seven or eight times for each person at the altar. They would keep positioning themselves in front of me and asking me to pray for them. When asked what I did during those meetings, my wife responded by saying, "Michael prays for people until nobody is moving, and then he grabs his briefcase and runs from the building." That was literally true. As long as I would pray for people, they continued to get in line to receive prayer.

When we felt it was time for us to close our part in the revival meetings, the pastor and his wife begged us not to leave. They were concerned if we left that Presence would leave. I told them, "Pastor, there is something about the hunger in your people that has attracted Him. He has declared He has chosen to dwell in this place. Unless you do something stupid, He will be here." For the next year, that pastor would ring me every two weeks or so. Almost every conversation began the same way. "Michael, He is still here." Sometime later a friend from New Zealand was preaching in that church. I needed to speak with him so I rang him. When he answered the phone, he asked me if I knew where he was at. I told him I knew he was in Paducah. That was not what he meant. "So, I asked, "Where are you." He responded, "I am sitting on the front row of the auditorium with Pastor, and Michael, He is still here."

In a twenty-week meeting in Lower Hutt, New Zealand, the Presence came and remained. One visiting pastor described the Presence by saying he "felt like he walked into a wall when he came into the building." A denominational executive, who had spent the night on his face, simply said, "God Himself has chosen to come to this place." In the following years, I watched guest speakers struggle to remain on their feet behind the pulpit because the Presence was so strong.

Not only must we prepare a place for Him, but we must prepare that place *"According to all that I shew thee."* I must come to God on His terms. I do not set the terms in this relationship. He says, "I will show you how to build this place for me." Notice the word "all." Partial obedience is actually disobedience. I am not trying to bring condemnation on the one who is struggling to live for Jesus, but I am saying that intentional sloppy Christian living won't cut it. Total surrender to Jesus…I must come to the place of repentance. I come to a place where I put my faith in Him…alone. I am not trusting any works that I can do. I am depending upon what He did at the cross for me. I asked a girl once if she was saved…if she was living for Jesus. She said "kinda" so I asked her if that was like being "kinda pregnant?" One cannot be kinda pregnant. You either are or you are not. I am surrendered to God or I am not. I urge you to make a total surrender to Him today.

This place we build for God is to be "*after the pattern.*" Are any of you ladies seamstresses? If she had time, my wife could be an excellent seamstress. Early in our marriage when she wanted to make a dress, she would buy a pattern to follow in making it. Now, it just looked like cloth and paper to me, but she knew if she wanted it to look right, she would be required to follow the pattern.

There is a pattern for salvation.

Step one is to ask Jesus to forgive you of your sins. This is to admit you have sinned. Most friends, who are reading this message will admit they have sinned, but Sir, if you do not believe you have sinned, let me speak to your wife. She can give me a list of your sins. And Ma'am the reverse is also true.

I must admit, I have sinned, and I must ask Him to forgive me.

This pattern for salvation includes believing Jesus is the Son of God and that He died to take the punishment for your sins. Jesus was totally man, but He was and is more than that. He is also the Son of God. God did become man so that man could be forgiven. To be saved today, you must believe that Jesus is both God and man and that His death was for you.

Then this pattern includes confessing Jesus as your Saviour. Romans 10:9,10,13 (KJV) puts it this way, "*That if thou shalt confess with thy mouth the Lord Jesus, and shalt believe in thine heart that God hath raised him from the dead, thou shalt be saved. For with the heart man believeth unto righteousness; and with the mouth confession is made unto salvation... For whosoever shall call upon the name of the Lord shall be saved.*" To call is to ask to be saved. To believe is to put your faith in Him. To confess is to say with your mouth what He says.

Church, there are patterns for revival as well. Hunger is required. Holiness is still important to Him. The habitation of His Presence...humility...harvest to name a few keys. These are the keys; these are the patterns that still bring revival.

If we were together in a church auditorium, I would say something like this, "Well, it is time for us to respond to the Lord today." Then I would give two opportunities. So I will close this chapter by doing exactly that.

First, I want to give an invitation to the reader who is not living for Jesus. Perhaps you have never given your life to Him. Perhaps you are backslidden, away from Him. You have lost your way. You once knew Him, but something has happened, and you are far away from Him now. It may be you are living in ways you know He does not want you to live. You are doing things you know Jesus would not do. The witness in your heart is that it is time for you to make things right with God.

I would invite you to pray this prayer with me. Make it the honest cry of your heart.

"Jesus, I admit I have sinned. I want to repent, that is, I want to turn away from my sin. Jesus, I want to ask You to forgive me for my sin. I have hurt You. I have hurt others. I have hurt myself. I am sorry. I ask You to forgive me. I believe You are the Son of God. I believe You came to this earth from heaven. I believe You were born of a virgin birth. I invite You into my life. I ask You to wash away my sin with Your blood. I believe that You said in John 1:12 if I would receive You I would become a child of God. I receive you now."

If you have prayed that prayer and surrendered your life to Jesus, I would love to hear about it. You can email me at mikliven@aol.com or go to mikelivengoodministries.com and share your story there by going to the contact page.

If you were in an auditorium where I was preaching, I would then give an invitation for those who would like to ask God to increase the hunger in their life as a believer.

Perhaps a great way for you to close this chapter would be to set aside some time and make a place for Him according to the pattern He will show you.

56

One of the simplest, yet most powerful, salvation messages I have preached comes from the book of Romans. The message is not new nor unique to me. I often heard it growing up. It is the bread and butter passage for personal soul winning. In fact, these are the passages I have often gone to in leading a person to Christ.

I have often used a simple prop of a can of cola or a cup of coffee when I share this message. I will simply set the can of cola or a cup of coffee on the podium in front of me. With that explanation, let's look at the Roman Road to Salvation, or How to Get to Heaven from Your City.

CHAPTER SIX

ROMAN ROAD TO SALVATION!
or
HOW TO GET TO HEAVEN FROM YOUR CITY

Instead of you thinking of me preaching a sermon today, I would like you to imagine that you and I are having a cup of coffee or a cola at your favorite coffee shop, and we are having a conversation about getting from your city to heaven!

Would you agree with me that your city may be great, but it is not heaven?

If we were having that cup of coffee, and we were discussing how we could get to heaven from your city, I would begin by taking you to the book of Romans. I would suggest we go to Romans 3:23. So let's do that.

Romans 3:23 (KJV) simply says, *"All have sinned, and come short of the glory of God."*

All have sinned! Just how many is all?

Does that include your Pastor? Does that include the person sitting next to you?

If you were in church with me, I would have you turn to the person sitting next to you and say, "Hello there, Sinner." Of course, while we were doing that, a lot of laughter would break out in the auditorium. I would probably say something like, "Some of you had way too much fun saying that."

I suppose I could have you turn to the person next to you on the train or plane and say, "Hello, Sinner," but that probably would not be a good idea.

Am I included in that all? Am I a sinner?

It is OK for you to declare that I am a sinner because that statement does include me.

All have sinned!

Sin basically comes in two packages, which I described in the previous chapter. The first package we could call the sins of commission. This is described in 1 John 3:4 (KJV), *"Whosoever committeth sin transgresseth also the law for sin is the transgression of the law."* This is basically breaking God's Word! It is stealing, telling a lie, adultery, etc. This is doing anything the Lord tells you not to do!

The second package we could call sins of omission. This is described in James 4:17 (KJV), *"Therefore to him that knoweth to do good, and doeth it not to him it is sin."* This is basically failing to keep God's law. This is not doing what you know you should do. This includes things like loving your enemy. One person said, "I am having trouble loving my friends, let alone my enemies."

To sin is to fall short of God's ideal…His expectation.

If we were having that cup of coffee or can of cola, I would probably ask you, "How many sins does it take to be a sinner?" Am I a sinner when I commit five sins? Or is ten sins the number of sins that I commit that causes me to be a sinner?

Perhaps a different illustration might help. How many stop signs do I have to run to be a law breaker? I was driving a van full of church folk home from a conference. The van was "acting up" a bit. It seemed every time we came to a stop the van would die. It would quit running. Around 12:30 in the morning, we were driving through this really small town. It only had one stop sign in the town, and nobody was awake in the town, so I did not come to a full stop at the single stop sign. I just kind of did a rolling stop.

Did I say nobody was awake in the town? It turned out there was one person awake after all. He had these special colored lights on his vehicle. I tried to explain about the van dying every time I stopped it . (which, by the way, it refused to do during my conversation with this gentleman). It turned out he believed that if I ran just one stop sign, I was a lawbreaker.

May I suggest all it takes to be a sinner is to have one sin in my life.

Have you ever told a lie? Have you ever said something you should not have said? Sir, have you ever watched a video you should not have watched?

If we were having that cup of coffee or can of cola, I suspect you would agree with me that you have certainly been guilty of one sin. In fact, I have never met anyone who, once they understood what sin is, would say to me, "Well, I do not have any sin in my life." No, I think we can agree I have sinned… your pastor has sinned…your neighbor has sinned…even you have sinned.

If we were having that cup of coffee or cola, and we had established that all of us have indeed sinned, I would turn to Romans 6:23. Here the Bible says, *"For the wages of sin is death; but the gift of God is eternal life through Jesus Christ our Lord"* (KJV).

Let's pause at that first phrase for a moment. *"For the wages of sin is death."* Do you work a job? If you don't have a job, would you like to have one?

If you are working a job, you understand a wage. It is what you receive for what you have done. Most of us would not go to work if we were not receiving a wage. You may be thinking,

59

"Yes, and I deserve even more than I am being paid." And I will be glad to agree with you.

May I say sin has a wage—those who have sinned earn something. That is, they have something coming to them.

"The wages of sin is death," but what does that mean?

Death is used three ways in Scripture. First, it describes physical death. Most of us understand physical death. We have been to a funeral service.

From Romans 5:12 we learn that death entered into the world because of one man—Adam's sin brought the curse of death upon all of us. Here is what the verse says, *"Wherefore, as by one man sin entered into the world, and death by sin; and so death passed upon all men, for that all have sinned"* (KJV). 1 Corinthians 15:21-22 makes it clear, again, that death came upon all of us because of Adam's sin. *"For since by man came death, by man came also the resurrection of the dead. For as in Adam all die, even so in Christ shall all be made alive"* (KJV).

Second, it describes spiritual death. Let's put down the coffee for a moment and read Ephesians 2:1 (KJV), *"And you hath he quickened, who were dead in trespasses and sins."* Obviously, they were not physically dead. If they were physically dead, they could not be reading this letter Paul had sent to them. So the Scripture means they were spiritually dead. I was reading this morning a Bible scholar who observed that death really means separation. At physical death our spirit and soul is separated from our body. At spiritual death our spirit and soul is separated from God. The life God has intended for you to experience on the inside is not there. You are not in fellowship with Him.

The third use of the word is to describe eternal death or eternal separation from God in hell. The result of sin is not only spiritual death, but it is eternal death! This is the ultimate consequence of sin.

This death is contrasted to the eternal life Jesus desires to give us. Adam's sin brought death into the human condition, but the death of Jesus brings the possibility of life.

The death for the one rejecting Christ is eternal! In Matthew 25:46 Jesus describes some who *"will go away into eternal punishment"* (KJV) and then contrasts them with *"the righteous"* who go *"into eternal life"* (NIV).

The back half of Romans 6:23 says, *"but the gift of God is eternal life through Jesus Christ our Lord."* Let me put a hold on that part for a moment. I will come back to it.

So far we have learned the Bible says that all of us, that is, every person who has ever drawn a breath, has sinned. Then, we learned that the consequence of sin is to be separated from God forever.

So far things do not look good!

So could I suggest we go to Romans 5:8 (KJV), *"But God commendeth His love toward us, in that, while we were yet sinners, Christ died for us."* Here is the greatest truth in God's Word. *"But God commendeth His love toward us."* You are incredibly loved by the Godhead.

You see, He does not want you to go to hell. He does not want to be eternally separated from you, but your sins have done exactly that. They have separated you and God.

The greatest expression of God's love for you is found in this statement. *"Christ died for us!"* Christ died for Michael Livengood. Go ahead and put your name there. Christ died for you.

If you were sitting next to someone in an auditorium and I was preaching, I would have them turn to you right now and say to you, "Christ died for you." You see, in His death Jesus took my punishment upon Himself — He took my place! In His death Jesus took your punishment upon Himself. Incredible love!

But I must understand, God is not only love, He is also holy and just. God cannot deny His nature. Justice will always require consequences for our actions. The Cross was God's way of balancing the demands of justice and the desire of love.

Notice the death occurred when we "were yet sinners." He did not love me when I was good. He loved me when I was

61

bad. He loved me when I was in rebellion. He loved me when I was a sinner. The concept behind the root word for sinner is one who has missed the mark and, therefore, cannot receive the prize. I remind you and myself again that Romans 3:23 says we have fallen short. We did not hit the mark. Think of the one shooting the arrow at the target, but coming short of the goal. That was us. We violated His Word. We were not reflections of His Glory. We have hurt others; we hurt Him; we have hurt ourselves. Yet, while we were in this condition He loved us.

If we were sitting here together drinking a cup of coffee or cola, I would let you know that you have a part in this story. You see, the gift of eternal life that I want to share with you is not automatic. We do play a part.

Our part is revealed in Romans 10:9,10,13 (KJV), *"That if thou shalt confess with thy mouth the Lord Jesus, and shalt believe in thine heart that God hath raised him from the dead, thou shalt be saved. For with the heart man believeth unto righteousness; and with the mouth confession is made unto salvation...For whosoever shall call upon the name of the Lord shall be saved."*

Our part is to believe in our heart that God raised Jesus from the dead. We believe or have faith in the Deity of Jesus. That is, I must believe that Jesus is God's Son. I must believe that in His death and burial, He was taking on Himself the punishment for my sin. He literally took my place on that cross. I should have been crucified. I should pay the price for my own sin. However, Jesus died for me. He took my sin on Himself.

I believe in my heart that He rose from the dead. The empty tomb is still there just outside of Jerusalem. His resurrection is the guarantee for your resurrection.

However, you do not stop with your heart, for with the mouth, confession is made unto salvation. Your mouth acknowledges what is in your heart! Usually, this includes admitting we have sinned. With my mouth I acknowledge I have sinned. With my mouth I acknowledge who Jesus is. I ask Him to allow His death and resurrection to cover my sin.

Romans 10:13 puts it in a very straightforward manner. *"Whosoever shall call upon the name of the Lord shall be saved."* Whosoever — that is you and me! Once again, if I was preaching I would have the person next to you turn to you and say, "Hello, Whosoever."

The promise to Whosoever is very clear — *"shall be saved."*

But Romans 10:13 says I have to *"call upon the name of the Lord."* Here is where I must tell you I cannot do that for you. The Lord cannot do that for you. You must call!

If you do, you will be saved.

What does it mean for you to be saved? Actually, you will spend the rest of your life coming to understand all the benefits of being saved, but here is a primary meaning of being saved. You get to receive the gift of God.

"What gift?" you say. Why, the gift of Romans 6:23 that I told you we would come back to, *"the gift of God is eternal life through Jesus Christ our Lord."* This is God's gift for you — eternal life!

Now, here would be a great place to ask you the most important question I could ask you over this cup of coffee, but before I ask that question, I do need to leave one more very important truth with you.

Jesus wants you to experience eternal life. The word *eternal* here does mean forever. Every reputable Greek scholar agrees with that.

You need to know Jesus used the same word in Matthew 25:46 to describe both the punishment of the wicked and the reward for the righteous. He said, *"And these shall go away into everlasting punishment: but the righteous into life eternal"* (KJV). In the Greek, the words for *everlasting* and *eternal* are the same word. If I believe that Heaven is forever, then I must also believe Hell is forever. The gift of God is forever, and the wages of sin are forever.

You can receive what you deserve…the wages of sin, or you can receive the gift of God…eternal life.

So, it we were sitting together having a cup of coffee, I would ask you three questions.

"Would you like to go to Heaven some day?" Then I would wait for your answer. I heard a former President of the United States say the most important thing for him was to know he was going to heaven. On the assumption you would say, "Yes, I would like to go to Heaven someday," I would ask you a second question.

"Are there any valid reasons why you should not ask Jesus into your life today?" On the assumption we would agree there are no valid reasons for you not to ask Jesus into your life, I would ask you one more question.

"Will you turn from your sins and ask Jesus to be your Saviour today? I will help you."

I closed the previous chapter with the following prayer and request:

"Jesus, I admit I have sinned. I want to repent, that is I want to turn away from my sin. Jesus, I want to ask You to forgive me for my sin. I have hurt You. I have hurt others. I have hurt myself. I am sorry. I ask You to forgive me. I believe You are the Son of God. I believe You came to this earth from heaven. I believe You were born of a virgin birth. I invite You into my life. I ask You to wash away my sin with Your blood. I believe that You said in John 1:12 if I would receive You, I would become a child of God. I receive you now."

If you have prayed that prayer and surrendered your life to Jesus, I would love to hear about it. You can email me at mikliven@aol.com, or go to mikelivengoodministries.com, and share your story there by going to the contact page.

64

The last two chapters have been fairly straight forward salvation messages. This message is another very simple salvation message, but I have found it really connects with the believer as well.

John 5: 31 (NIV), "If I testify about myself, my testimony is not valid.

32 There is another who testifies in my favour, and I know that his testimony about me is valid.

33 "You have sent to John and he has testified to the truth.

34 Not that I accept human testimony; but I mention it that you may be saved.

35 John was a lamp that burned and gave light, and you chose for a time to enjoy his light.

36 "I have testimony weightier than that of John. For the very work that the Father has given me to finish, and which I am doing, testifies that the Father has sent me.

37 And the Father who sent me has himself testified concerning me. You have never heard his voice nor seen his form,

38 nor does his word dwell in you, for you do not believe the one he sent.

39 You diligently study the Scriptures because you think that by them you possess eternal life. These are the Scriptures that testify about me,

40 yet you refuse to come to me to have life.

CHAPTER SEVEN

FOUR WITNESSES

The court system in most western nations, before the advent of DNA, was based on the word of the witness. Rarely was someone convicted without a personal witness against them.

Jesus made some incredible claims about Himself. He claimed to be the Son of God—the promised Messiah for the Jewish nation. If He is the Son of God, then it is essential I relate properly to Him.

Some time back I was invited to speak to a Christian group at Southern Illinois University. I spoke on the proofs of the resurrection of Jesus from the dead. The next night I was speaking at a local church, and a young man from Japan, who had attended the lecture at the university, was in attendance. At the close of my message that evening, he wanted to talk with me. He said, "Sir, I have been thinking about what you said yesterday. I have come to the conclusion that you are correct. The evidence says that Jesus Christ rose from the dead. If He rose from the dead, then I must commit my life to Him. I really do not have any choice. If He rose from the dead, then He is who He said He was."

I am going to ask you to commit your life to this Jesus just like that student from Japan. At the close of this chapter, I am going to give you an opportunity to give your life to Him. I am going to ask you to radically surrender your life to Jesus.

But before I would ask you to do that, is there evidence to support these claims Jesus made about Himself? Are there witnesses to validate this claim? Certainly many people have made claims to be a messiah—a god—over the years. Every generation seems to produce its own version of a human claiming to be more than a human.

Are there witnesses?

I believe witnesses do exist. I would like us to examine four witnesses to this claim Jesus made.

The Testimony of Your Friends

I would like us to go to the Gospel of John, chapter number one and verse twenty-nine. We will read through verse thirty-four. *"The next day John saw Jesus coming toward him and said, 'Look, the Lamb of God, who takes away the sin of the world! This is*

66

the one I meant when I said, 'A man who comes after me has surpassed me because he was before me.' I myself did not know him, but the reason I came baptizing with water was that he might be revealed to Israel.' Then John gave this testimony: 'I saw the Spirit come down from heaven as a dove and remain on him. I would not have known him, except that the one who sent me to baptize with water told me, 'The man on whom you see the Spirit come down and remain is he who will baptize with the Holy Spirit.' I have seen and I testify that this is the Son of God'." (NIV)

John was a man on a mission. He understood his call was to introduce the Messiah. He had been sent to introduce Him to the world. John was not going to be easily deceived. He knew his assignment. He knew how important it was that he get it right. He would need to be convinced by the evidence.

What does John say?

"He was before me." From the human perspective John the Baptist was six months older than Jesus, but John understood that Jesus was more than just a man. He knew Jesus existed before John was born.

John described his mission, *"I came baptizing that He might be revealed."* This was his purpose: that Jesus might be revealed. And that is the purpose of this message…of this chapter…that Jesus might be revealed.

John's purpose was revelatory based on a supernatural event. *"The One who sent me…told me."* John, you will see the Holy Spirit descend and remain on someone. That someone will be the One you are looking for.

May I suggest John represents your friends?

We accept the witness of our friends on many things. Some of you are married to a person you met on a blind date. Perhaps, like me, you married someone you were introduced to by a friend.

Perhaps you have bought something because a friend recommended it. Perhaps you have gone to watch a movie or tuned in a particular TV program because a friend said it was good. I am sure many of us tried a certain restaurant because a friend recommended it to us.

67

Well, I would like you to consider the witness of your friend who has been talking to you about Jesus. Perhaps it is the friend who gave you this book. They have been saying to you that Jesus is the Son of God. They have been encouraging you to give your life to Him. Perhaps they have asked you directly to let them pray with you to receive Jesus. You have trusted their advice on other areas. Let me encourage you to trust them on this one.

The Works That I Do Testify

Not only do your friends witness to you that Jesus is the Christ, the Son of God, but the works that Jesus did also point to who He is.

First consider that **the life** of Jesus testifies of Him. Certainly Pilate, the Roman political leader, could find no fault in Him. At His trial Pilate could find no sin…no wrong in Him.

Do you realize all of time is divided between BC and AD? BC stands for Before Christ and AD is for Anno Domino, the Year of the Lord. He really is the central figure in mankind's history. He needs to be the central figure in your life.

Secondly, **the miracles** that Jesus did speak to the fact that He is the Son of God. Nicodemus understood that. Listen to his account in John 3:1-2 (NIV).

"Now there was a man of the Pharisees named Nicodemus, a member of the Jewish ruling council. He came to Jesus at night and said, 'Rabbi, we know you are a teacher who has come from God. For no -one could perform the miraculous signs you are doing if God were not with him'."

In fact, the entire Gospel of John is a book revealing the signs and wonders that Jesus did.

Not only did the wonders reveal who He was, but **the teachings** of Jesus also revealed who He was, as well. Jesus had an incredible encounter with a woman at a well. As a result of that encounter, she became convinced Jesus was the Saviour. She excitedly shared her experience with the people of her city. They, too, listened to Jesus.

In John 4:42 The people of the town said to the woman, *"We no longer believe just because of what you said; now we have heard for ourselves, and we know that this man really is the Saviour of the world."* (NIV)

Have you really considered what He said? His teachings separate Him from all others. One of those sent to arrest Jesus came back and said, *"No one ever spoke the way this man does,"* (John 7:46 NIV).

Then, **the resurrection** of Jesus from the dead declares He is the Son of God. May I say, Christianity stands or falls with the resurrection. If He arose from the dead, it substantiates His claims. If He did not, it debunks Him.

Not only did Jesus do the great works, but He still does them. Consider some works that Jesus still does.

Jesus is still changing lives. Some of you have friends whose lives were forever changed by an encounter with Jesus. Some of you are the ones whose lives were forever changed.

Jesus is still doing miraculous healings. Some of you have been healed.

I can testify of many healings. Let me share three with you.

My younger brother had been diagnosed with rickets, the bone disease. The doctor told my parents that you could pop this boy's head like a ping pong ball. He was taken by our parents to a tent meeting where an evangelist prayed for my brother, and God healed him. I can testify there is nothing wrong with his bones. We have banged heads on the basketball court many times, and his head is hard.

I am thinking of the girl at a kid's camp in Nebraska. I felt we should do prayer tunnels. I had all the girls go through one line and all the boys went through another. The girls' line was experiencing an anointing of the Spirit. The boys' line was having a fist fight. So I am in the back of the auditorium breaking up a fight and thinking this prayer tunnel idea was not a good idea. Then one of the lady counselors came to me and excitedly told me that God had just healed this little girl of scoliosis. I asked how she knew. I sent her to the camp nurse. She told me I cannot do a proper physical here, but I cannot detect any curvature in her spine. Two weeks later the camp director spoke at the church the little girl attended. She was met by the girl's mother who, with tears in her eyes, described the healing that indeed had happened. The plan had been for daughter to be placed in a back brace that she would be required to wear the rest of her life. But God did intervene. The scoliosis was gone. She will never need to wear this back brace. Jesus healed her.

In a church in Texas, the pastor told the people that I was going to prophesy over the entire church, which was the first I heard of it. My first thought, was, "Pastor, do not worry about retirement because you are not going to live that long. I am going to kill you personally after this service is over."

I found myself standing in front of a lady. As I stood there, I heard myself say to her, "You will never need to fear dying of cancer for the LORD is saying to you, 'You will never die of cancer.' " As this was coming out of my mouth, I was thinking to myself, "Shut up, Michael. Just shut up."

A year later I was speaking at that church, and the pastor said, "I have a testimony you need to hear." This dear lady began to share how she had been diagnosed with cancer. The prognosis was not good. Plans were being made for her funeral when she heard the LORD say to her, "What did I tell you?" The long story short is that He did heal her. But there is more. At least twice since then, she has been diagnosed with cancer, and twice the LORD has healed her.

Some reading this chapter have even been healed by Jesus.

I would like you to consider that these works tell us Jesus is more than a man. You can come to Him today as Saviour and Healer.

The Testimony of the Father

John the Baptist will testify that Jesus is the Son of God. The works of Jesus testify that He is the Son of God. But we can bring another witness to the stand.

Three times the Father spoke from heaven regarding Jesus. The first occurred at the baptism of Jesus. A second takes place in John 12:28-30. *"'Father, glorify your name!' Then a voice came from heaven, 'I have glorified it, and will glorify it again'...Jesus said, 'This voice was for your benefit, not mine'"* (NIV).

The third is found in Matthew 17:5-6 on the Mount of Transfiguration. *"While he was still speaking, a bright cloud covered them, and a voice from the cloud said, 'This is my Son, whom I love; with him I am well pleased. Listen to him!' When the disciples heard this, they fell facedown to the ground, terrified"* (NIV).

The Father, by the Spirit, is still testifying today. Here is what 1 John 5: 6-9 declares, *"This is the one who came by water and blood – Jesus Christ. He did not come by water only, but by water and blood. And it is the Spirit who testifies, because the Spirit is the truth. For there are three that testify: the Spirit, the water and the blood; and the three are in agreement. We accept man's testimony, but God's testimony is greater because it is the testimony of God, which he has given about his Son"* (NIV).

Jesus made reference to the ongoing witness of the Holy Spirit regarding Himself in John 16:7-13, *"But very truly I tell you, it is for your good that I am going away. Unless I go away, the Advocate will not come to you; but if I go, I will send him to you. When he comes, he will prove the world to be in the wrong about sin and righteousness and judgment: about sin, because people do not believe in me; about righteousness, because I am going to the Father, where you can see me no longer; and about judgment, because the prince of this world now stands condemned. I have much more to say to you, more than you can now bear. But when he, the Spirit of truth, comes, he will guide you into all the truth. He will not speak on his own; he will speak only what he hears, and he will tell you what is yet to come"* (NIV).

Many of you can recall how the Spirit began to convict you of sin and of the reality of Jesus. He may have orchestrated circumstances in your life, but the day also came when He began to speak to your heart, as well.

I believe others are aware the Holy Spirit is speaking to your heart today, even as you are reading these words. Something within you says, "Yes I know Jesus is who He says He is." Something within you says, "Yes I have sin in my life." Something within you says, "Yes I need to give my life to Him." That something is actually not a something but a Someone. That Someone is the Holy Spirit. Will you listen to that voice today? I actually plead with you to do so.

The Scripture Bears Witness To Jesus

The purpose of John's Gospel is found in John 20:30, *"Jesus performed many other signs in the presence of his disciples, which are not recorded in this book. But these are written that you may believe that Jesus is the Messiah, the Son of God, and that by believing you may have life in his name"* (NIV).

Here, we have another reference to the works, the miraculous signs Jesus did, but please notice the "why" of the Bible, *"These are written that you may believe."* This book is a record of Jesus.

I was preaching in an Illinois community where a man who was somewhat skeptical of the Gospel was in attendance. During a brief conversation with Him, I felt led to challenge him to simply read the Gospel of John. He was a skeptic, but he was an honest skeptic, and he agreed to do so. He made a decision if he was going to read the Gospel he would read it out loud and dramatize the parts. He returned to the service the following night. In another brief conversation, he explained to me that something was happening inside of him as he was reading the book of John. I simply encouraged him to continue reading. Within a few days, he came to a saving faith in Jesus.

May I say that every book of the Bible actually points to Jesus!

In Genesis He is the Seed of the woman.

In Exodus He is the Passover Lamb.

In Leviticus He is the Pillar of Cloud by Day and the Pillar of Fire by Night.

In Numbers He is our High Priest.

And Deuteronomy describes Him as the Prophet like unto Moses.

Joshua reveals Him as the Captain of our Salvation.

And Judges reveals Him as our Judge and Lawgiver.

Ruth reveals Him as our Kinsman Redeemer.

And 1 & 2 Samuel reveal Him as our Trusted Prophet.

In the books of Kings and Chronicles He is our Reigning King.

In Ezra He is our Faithful Scribe.

In Nehemiah He is the Rebuilder of the broken down walls of human lives.

And in Esther He is our Mordecai.

Job portrays Him as the Redeemer who ever lives and my Dayspring from on High.

While Psalms portrays Him as the Shepherd.

Proverbs and Ecclesiastes portray Him as our Lover and Bridegroom.

The prophet Isaiah calls Him the Prince of Peace.

Jeremiah calls Him the Righteous Branch.

While the book of Lamentations pictures Him as the Weeping Prophet.

Ezekiel sees Him as the Wonderful Four-Faced Man.

In Daniel He is found to be the Fourth Man in the Fire.

Hosea says He is forever married to the backslider.

Joel prophesizes He is the Baptizer in the Holy Spirit.

Amos knows Him as the Burden Bearer.

And Obadiah sees Him as the Holy and Righteous Deliverer.

Jonah teaches He is the Foreign Missionary.

And Micah sees Him as the Messenger with Beautiful Feet.

In Nahum He is a Stronghold in the day of trouble.

In Habakkuk He is the Prophet crying revive thy work in the midst of the years.

In Zephaniah He is Mighty to Save.

and In Haggai He is the Restorer of God's lost heritage.

Zechariah sees Him as the Fountain opened in the House of David for sin and unrighteousness.

Malachi closes out the Old Testament by saying Jesus is The Lord rising with healing in His wings.

The witness continues in the New Testament for:

In Matthew He is the Messiah.

In Mark He is the Wonder Worker.

In Luke He is the Son of Man.

But in John He is also the Son of God.

In the book of Acts He is seen in the work of the Holy Spirit.

In Romans He is our Justifier.

And in 1 & 2 Corinthians He is our Sanctifier.

In Galatians He is the Redeemer from the curse of the Law.

In Ephesians He is the Christ of the unsearchable riches.

Philippians reveals Him as the Supplier of all that we have need of.

Colossians says He is the fullness of the Godhead bodily.

In 1 & 2 Thessalonians He is our Coming King.

In 1 & 2 Timothy He is our Mediator between God and man.

In Titus He is our Faithful Pastor.

While in Philemon He is our Friend who is closer than a brother.

Hebrews says He is the Blood of a Better Covenant.

James calls Him our Great Physician.

1 & 2 Peter reveal Him as a Great Shepherd.

The Epistles of John simply reveal Him as Love.

Jude announces Him as The Lord coming with ten thousands of His saints.

Revelation wraps this testimony up by revealing He is King of Kings and Lord of Lords.

The Apostle Paul, who may have known Jesus more intimately than any other person, stands before Felix the Governor in Acts 24:25. *"As Paul talked about righteousness, self-control and the judgment to come, Felix was afraid"* (NIV). Felix becomes aware of his sin and, in truth, he who was the judge is now being judged.

How Will You Respond?

Today, these witnesses still proclaim Jesus is the Christ... the Son of God.

When He was on the earth in His human form, He called people to follow Him. He still calls people to follow Him. He calls you to follow Him.

But now the question is, how will you respond?

Will you join with my young friend from Japan in a full surrender of your life to Jesus Christ?

If we were together in an auditorium I would be inviting you to indicate your full surrender to Jesus by leaving your seat and walking to the front of the auditorium where we would pray together a prayer inviting the Son of God into your life. You can pray that prayer right where you are right now. I invite you to pray the following prayer.

"Jesus, I admit I have sinned. I want to repent, that is I want to turn away from my sin. Jesus, I want to ask You to forgive me for my sin. I have hurt You. I have hurt others. I have hurt myself. I am sorry. I ask You to forgive me. I believe You are the Son of God. I believe You came to this earth from heaven. I believe You were born of a virgin birth. I invite You into my life. I ask You to wash away my sin with Your blood. I believe that You said in John 1:12 if I would receive You, I would become a child of God. I receive you now."

If you have prayed that prayer and surrendered your life to Jesus, I would love to hear about it. You can email me at mikliven@aol.com, or go to mikelivengoodministries.com and share your story there by going to the contact page.

This message began as I saw a parallel between events related to the first coming of Jesus and the second coming that is prophesied. It is very much a revival-related message, with emphasis on salvation, sanctification, and baptism in the Spirit.

Luke 3:16-17, John answered, saying unto them all, I indeed baptize you with water; but one mightier than I cometh, the latches of whose shoes I am not worthy to unloose: he shall baptize you with the Holy Ghost and with fire: Whose fan is in his hand, and he will throughly purge his floor, and will gather the wheat into his garner; but the chaff he will burn with fire unquenchable. (KJV)

CHAPTER EIGHT

FOUR TRADEMARKS OF THE LAST-DAY REVIVAL

Throughout Scripture it seemed whenever the Lord God was getting ready to do something truly significant, He liked to drop hints in advance. I believe He still likes to do that. Sometimes those hints are in your own heart; you have a word from Him that something is about to happen, and you will never be the same.

A Midwest Deacon shared with me that just a few weeks before a 15-week revival broke out in his church, God began preparing him. He described an encounter in his lounge where the Spirit of the Lord seemed to come in such a heavy way that he was literally unable to move out of his chair. The explanation of the Spirit was that God was preparing to send a revival that would change his life forever...and it happened!

Sometimes those hints come in the form of prophetic activity or an increase of God activity in the church. The spiritual atmosphere seems to be building. Expectation of something arises.

Scripture says, *"In the fullness of time God would send His Son"* (Galatians 4:4 KJV). I love that thought. Heaven does not move by accident. God's plans and purposes will be accomplished. However, before God sent that Son He sent a messenger—the voice of one in the wilderness crying out, "Get ready the Lord is coming!"

As John the Baptist proclaimed the Messiah was about to make His appearance, he does three things.

First, he tells them who is coming. *"One mightier than I."* I could just camp at that thought for a bit. As a messenger, I must understand I am not the message, for the One who is mightier is coming.

John continues with this statement, *"whose shoes I am not worthy to unloose."* I need to catch that. You need to catch that. You see servants are not glorified. When people began to come to John to tell him that *"all men"* are going to Jesus, John responds with some of the most incredible words in Scripture. *"He must increase, but I must decrease"* — (John 3:30 KJV).

There was no place for jealousy. John understood his role. This is the pattern for us to follow. May they see Jesus rather than seeing us. I could wax eloquent on this thought. When Saul was little in his own eyes, God could use him. When he became arrogant, his days were numbered. Of course, we know Jesus is to be exalted, and we are to serve. Yet, the subtle temptation is still there to think it is our ministry...our position...we can slowly become the center of the message.

John tells them how to get ready for that coming. The message he preached involved repentance. The reality is that repentance may not make you popular with everyone. It cost John the Baptist his head.

Repentance involves three things. It includes admitting I am wrong. Hey guys, that is a reality. He is right, and we are wrong. As one born in the States who travels internationally, I often, to break ice, will tell other nations you can tell an American anything, except that he is wrong. I have pointed out certain politicians as classic examples of that. Once the chuckling dies down, I will then observe, it is not only Americans who have an issue with that challenge. Pride keeps us from admitting our sin. However, the reality is, I still have sinned. I was wrong. Repentance requires me to admit that.

Second, repentance involves turning away from my sin. Admission of sin is not enough. I must make the decision to turn away from the sin. I do not repent of my past so that I can continue to do the same sin. In repentance, I am making a decision to turn away from the sin. You see, I was wrong to think the sin was not wrong.

Repentance involves still one more thing. I not only turn away from sin, but then, I turn to the Lord. Sin prevents me from having a relationship with the Lord. For more confirmation of that, consider that it was sin that destroyed the relationship between Adam, Eve, and God Almighty. But, just stopping the sin does not give me a relationship with the Lord. I must turn to Him. Repentance was necessary because they were not ready… and, in our present condition, we are not ready…for His coming.

As the forerunner, John then tells the people of his day what would happen when Jesus comes. Four things are mentioned.

First, He will *"baptize you with the Holy Spirit and with fire"* (NIV). A one word definition of that is <u>RENEWAL</u>.

Second, He will *"clear his threshing-floor"* (NIV) or as the KJV says *"thoroughly purge his floor."* The one word definition for that is <u>REVIVAL</u>.

Number three, [He] will *"gather the wheat into his garner"* or *"barn."* May I suggest <u>REFORMATION</u> is being described here.

The last thing John says will happen is that Jesus will *"burn up the chaff with unquenchable fire"* (NIV). That, my friend, is <u>JUDGMENT</u>.

The same pattern is often evident in significant outpourings of God's Spirit or during times of God encounters. I also believe this is the pattern that will be in play just prior to the return of the Lord.

What are the types of things you can expect to see God do in you and around you in such seasons of God activity that have been given the name revival or outpouring? Let's explore those four statements a bit further to see what the hints are.

Renewal

John indicated one of the significant things Jesus will do is baptize people with the Holy Ghost and fire. I suggest this includes renewal.

The baptism in the Holy Spirit is a promised gift to all believers. I believe it is the greatest gift one can receive after salvation. Let me put it this way. Salvation is the greatest gift God has for the sinner, and the baptism in the Holy Spirit is the greatest gift God has for the child of God. There really is more, so do not stop with salvation. Press in for the baptism in the Spirit.

Scripture suggests two purposes for this baptism. The first purpose is to give you power for effective service. The second is power for holy living.

You can receive this gift today. In one service in the Philippine Islands where I was the preacher, over 300 were baptized in the Spirit. At a pre-teen camp in Indiana, 127 received this precious gift in one night. In a 19-week series of meetings we preached in New Zealand in 2008, the associate pastor said he had "never seen it so easy for people to receive the baptism in the Holy Spirit." For those who have not received this gift yet, I encourage you to ask the Lord to fill you.

However, I don't think I do too much injustice to the passage if I suggest renewal is not limited to the baptism in the Holy Spirit. The text says Holy Spirit and with fire. *The Dake's Annotated Reference Bible* observes that the emblem of fire represents zeal. We read in Psalm 104:4, *"He makes winds his messengers, flames of fire his servants"* (NIV). John 2:17 proclaims,

"His disciples remembered that it is written: 'Zeal for your house consumes me'" (NIV).

I have observed that the fruit of previous God moments includes a fresh zeal which comes. Sometimes the fire is almost literal, or at least it feels like a fire lit inside.

Revival

John said Jesus would purge His floor. Purging has to do with purifying and holiness. One work of revival is this purging and purifying. The NKJV of our text says, *"and He will thoroughly clean out His threshing floor."* The NAS says, *"thoroughly clear His threshing floor."* Let's consider this word *"thoroughly"* or *"throughly"* (KJV). This particular Greek word only appears here and in the parallel passage in Matthew 3. According to *Strong's Concordance,* the word means to *"cleanse perfectly."* According to *Thayer's Greek-English Lexicon* the meaning is to *"cleanse thoroughly."*

How long will God continue to call us to repentance? He will do this until He has cleansed every spot or blemish within us. He will continue to call us to repentance until He has prepared us for the work He wants to do through us.

It is so important not to get offended at the message of repentance. Rather, we must respond to it. We must allow the Lord to do the complete work He is wanting to do within us. The discipline may not be pleasant at first, but it will bring good fruit into your life.

It is possible there are those reading this chapter who will experience a conviction of the Holy Spirit concerning areas He wants to make clean. I have no interest in legalism, but I believe holiness will happen. This holiness includes a desire to walk as close and as clean before Jesus as possible.

Space will not permit the many stories about this cleansing, but let me tell you just one. I walked into a church office one morning to have the staff tell me they had seen the greatest miracle of their lives the previous night. I tried to think of

81

something that had happened that could qualify as the greatest miracle they had ever seen. Nothing would come to my mind. I walked into the pastor's office to hear the same thing. The previous night he had seen the greatest miracle he had ever seen. I finally said, "Pastor, it is obvious I am the only person who does not realize what God did last night." He went on to describe the gray-haired lady who had lain on the floor so long and so quiet that we thought she may have died. In fact, at one point he had placed his ear close to her mouth and nose to see if she was still breathing. Deep repentance had taken place. This lady, who had a reputation as the meanest woman in the valley, had already come into the church office earlier that morning to see what she needed to do to make things right with those she had deeply hurt over the years. In the following years, people talked about the radical change in her life.

The text suggests those who will not allow the cleansing or the changing will be swept away. Please understand, not everybody who says they are believers really are. As I bring this section to a close, let me say holiness is a major concern to God.

Reformation

Renewal and revival are not the finished project. Jesus will gather the wheat into the barn. I would like to call this reformation. Reformation, first of all, speaks to me of a major harvest. *Harvest* is a term that Scripture often uses in reference to souls. Consider these verses:

Matthew 9:37-38, *"Then he said to his disciple, 'The harvest is plentiful but the workers are few. Ask the Lord of the harvest, therefore, to send out workers into his harvest field"* (NIV).

Matthew 13:30, *"Let both grow together until the harvest. At that time I will tell the harvesters: First collect the weeds and tie them in bundles to be burned; then gather the wheat and bring it into my barn'"* (NIV).

Matthew 13:39, *"and the enemy who sows them is the devil. The harvest is the end of the age, and the harvesters are angels"* (NIV).

John 4:35, *"Do you not say, 'Four months more and then the harvest'? I tell you, open your eyes and look at the fields! They are ripe for harvest"* (NIV).

Romans 1:13, *"I do not want you to be unaware, brothers, that I planned many times to come to you (but have been prevented from doing so until now) in order that I might have a harvest among you, just as I have had among the other Gentiles"* (NIV).

Revelation 14:15, *"Then another angel came out of the temple and called in a loud voice to him who was sitting on the cloud, 'Take your sickle and reap, because the time to reap has come, for the harvest of the earth is ripe'"* (NIV).

As the Lord clears His floor, and it is His floor, and He does the cleaning, it is to prepare the floor to receive the abundant harvest He is going to send. The Lord has never lost sight of the harvest. In every significant visitation from God, the number of people getting saved increases and the passion for the lost increases, as well.

Following fifteen weeks of services where nearly 500 people had responded to a salvation altar call, the pastor observed the passion in his people for the lost had intensified. He knew beyond the immediate fruit that passion would lead to longterm fruit in the church.

Second, it speaks to me of the end of time. The harvest comes at the end of the farming season.

Judgment

Following this reformation, Jesus will burn the chaff with unquenchable fire. However, this time it is the fire of judgment. The fire of purging is to clean His bride, but this fire is a fire of judgment.

The chaff was that which sometimes grew alongside the wheat. In its early stages, the chaff could not be distinguished from the wheat. It looked like wheat, but it was not wheat.

Not everyone who says they are saved is saved. So I must ask you, "Are you saved?"

I don't say that to create bad feelings, but I want to be honest. And I am asking the Holy Spirit to make some readers uncomfortable. I want Him to bring conviction, on those who are not right with God.

God is cleaning up His church—will you let Him clean you up?

It appears the harvest is getting larger than ever—will you continue to go after the harvest in your city?

Judgment will come—I do not know when but I know it will happen...we have a season to respond to the Lord.

If I were preaching this message to a live audience in an auditorium, I would be calling for multiple responses. First, I would be calling to repentance and salvation those who are away from the Lord. Philippians 2:12 calls us to *"work out your own salvation with fear and trembling"* (ESV). This is not a salvation by personal works. We understand and teach salvation is an act of God's grace. But there is an outworking of this salvation. When Jesus comes into our lives, sin begins to lose its control.

This truth is brought home to our hearts in 1 John 3:4-10, *"Everyone who makes a practice of sinning also practices lawlessness; sin is lawlessness. You know that he appeared in order to take away sins, and in him there is no sin. No one who abides in him keeps on sinning; no one who keeps on sinning has either seen him or known him. Little children, let no one deceive you. Whoever practices righteousness is righteous, as he is righteous. Whoever makes a practice of sinning is of the devil, for the devil has been sinning from the beginning. The reason the Son of God appeared was to destroy the works of the devil. No one born of God makes a practice of sinning, for God's seed abides in him; and he cannot keep on sinning, because he has been born of God. By this it is evident who are the children of God, and who are the children of the devil: whoever does not practice righteousness is not of God, nor is the one who does not love his brother"* (ESV).

If I am living in sin, it is probably a good indication I am not really saved. Key word in this passage is *"practice."* If you are continuing to do sinful things after praying to receive Christ, you do not know Him. Full stop.

My first call if I was preaching in an auditorium would be to those who do not know Jesus or are backslidden. I would extend that net to those who are doing things that Jesus would not do. I would not overlook those who are religious but not right with God. You see, going to church does not make you a Christian any more than going into a garage makes you a car.

But the invitation would be extended further. I would call for sanctification. I would be calling for Christians to allow the work of the Spirit to bring a fresh purity to their lives. Will you take this opportunity to shut yourself in with the Holy Spirit and allow Him to evaluate your life? Let Him search out your actions, your attitudes, your relationships, your entertainment, and so forth.

Revival is not just about people getting saved. It is about purging our lives as believers.

I would also be calling for people to become filled with the Spirit. We would be praying for people accordingly.

In most revival services, we have time to pray for the fire of God to come.

These are the calls I would extend to them, and I encourage you to go after more of the Lord. Don't stop with the Cross. Go on to Pentecost!

Below is a prayer that has closed many of the chapters in this book.

"Jesus, I admit I have sinned. I want to repent; that is, I want to turn away from my sin. Jesus, I want to ask You to forgive me for my sin. I have hurt You. I have hurt others. I have hurt myself. I am sorry. I ask You to forgive me. I believe You are the Son of God. I believe You came to this earth from heaven. I believe You were born of a virgin birth. I invite You into my life. I ask You to wash away my sin with Your blood. I believe that You said in John 1:12 if I would receive You I would become a child of God. I receive you now."

If you have prayed that prayer and surrendered your life to Jesus I would love to hear about it. You can email me at mikliven@aol.com, or go to mikelivengoodministries.com and share your story there by going to the contact page.

The message in this chapter was first delivered during a 17-week Outpouring of the Spirit in Lower Hutt, New Zealand. I ministered at a "round-robin" event that was co-sponsored by five churches in Hutt Valley. Each night for those 17 weeks, I preached at a different one of those five churches. The message in this chapter was actually delivered at a combined meeting where all five churches came together for one service. Basically, I have viewed this message as a prophetic word from the LORD for the nation of New Zealand. With only one exception, the only nation where I have delivered this message is New Zealand. I actually hesitated to include the message because I felt it was so narrowly focused in its intent.

I have included it for three reasons. First, because it serves as an example of a prophetic type of message, a "thus saith the Lord," that, at some point, needs to be a part of revival. Second, because I am aware this book will make its way into the hands of a number of Kiwis. Third, I do believe that while the message was a word from God for the church of the Hutt Valley and the church of New Zealand, it does share Biblical principles that go beyond the New Zealand church.

Joel 2:12-17, Therefore also now, saith the LORD, turn ye even to me with all your heart, and with fasting, and with weeping, and with mourning:
13 And rend your heart, and not your garments, and turn unto the LORD your God: for he is gracious and merciful, slow to anger, and of great kindness, and repenteth him of the evil.
14 Who knoweth if he will return and repent, and leave a blessing behind him; even a meat offering and a drink offering unto the LORD your God?
15 Blow the trumpet in Zion, sanctify a fast, call a solemn assembly:

16 Gather the people, sanctify the congregation, assemble the elders, gather the children, and those that suck the breasts: let the bridegroom go forth of his chamber, and the bride out of her closet.

17 Let the priests, the ministers of the LORD, weep between the porch and the altar, and let them say, Spare thy people, O LORD, and give not thine heritage to reproach, that the heathen should rule over them: wherefore should they say among the people, Where is their God? (KJV)

CHAPTER NINE

A TIME TO REND YOUR HEART
or
A WORD FROM GOD ABOUT
REVIVAL IN NEW ZEALAND

In March of 2000 as we flew from the States to New Zealand, I began to feel as if the Lord were impressing a word upon my heart for the nation of New Zealand. I do not say that flippantly...or easily. I cannot say that I had ever had that type of sense in my heart before.

Occasionally that year, I would share that word as I felt I was supposed to, but by and large, I was reluctant to approach the topic. While preparing for this week of ministry, I began to sense perhaps this night was an occasion where I should share this word. In fact, I awakened this morning with it burning in my heart, and I feel somewhat compelled to share it.

Some people gravitate toward the title of *prophet*. They like the thought of being "a prophet of God." Some have probably called themselves prophets who in fact are not, and there is a difference in giving a prophecy and being a prophet.

I confess to having mixed emotions in this whole area. The fellowship I grew up in gave lip service to the concept of the existence of prophets today, but would have been very reluctant to recognize someone as a prophet. From time to time I have been approached by someone with a word about myself and the prophetic ministry. And that has often made me somewhat uncomfortable. At the same time I have a fascination with the unknown prophet motif. This is the one who comes in unannounced and unknown, delivers a word from God, and disappears again.

I have been doing an on-and-off-again study of the ministry of the prophet for some time now. At times I think I see anointings on my life that are similar to those of the prophet. At other times I am sure there are many of the signs of a prophet that are lacking in my life.

Having said that, I feel like tonight may be a prophetic word—more than a sermon but a word from the Lord. I am going to share with you what I feel the Lord burned into my heart in 2000 as we flew from the States to New Zealand for a six-week ministry tour. After I share the exact word I felt then, I am going to expand on it slightly. I want to make clear the difference between the exact words that I believe the Lord gave to me and my interpretation of them. Then, I am going to allow opportunity for you to respond to what you hear from the Lord.

Own Your Own Revival

The first thing I believe the Lord was saying to me on that flight was to say to you, "Take ownership of your own revival."

I believe that includes the thought of not looking to someone else to bring revival into New Zealand. As I observed New Zealanders in the early days of ministering in this nation, I noticed that you were not afraid to learn from others. By and large, that is good. However, the danger is going to be to simply try to duplicate that which they are doing rather than hearing from God for your own outpouring.

One of my honest reactions to that was, "Then why am I here preaching these revival-type services? It seemed contradictory to me. I did not have a clear answer in my heart to that question. It just seems that at this time Linda and I have been led to be here. I do know I want to be used of God to bring in significant revivals. I do know God has given us powerful and repeated promises and assignments related to revival. Still, I sense I must say to you "take ownership of your own revival."

I interpret that to include the following. Do not expect God to bring in revival from somewhere else, even as you do allow Him to encourage and bless you through ministries from other places He will send to you. Revival must take hold in your heart. Is it possible others want revival for you more than you want it for yourself?

You must own revival. One of the principles of leadership that a good leader understands is that if an idea is going to fly, the people must own it. That is they must buy into it…accept it as their own…be consumed by it. Revival leading to the transformation of your city must become a part of your fiber. If it is just a nice idea, it will not happen. John Knox was known to pray, "Give me Scotland, or I die." I am not saying every person in the city must feel this way but I am saying a nucleus must be gripped by it. Will you be a part of that nucleus?

Now let me give you two practics on owning your own revival. This will involve your personal prayer and intercession. Not all are called and gifted as intercessors, but all must intercede. I want to challenge you to regularly give time to praying for revival in New Zealand. Second, this will involve your personal witnessing…your personal evangelism or working for Jesus. Not all are called as evangelists. Not all will travel and preach. Not all may be gifted spiritual salesmen. But all must witness. All must share their part of the story. Minimally, you can commit to inviting people to church meetings.

Rend Your Heart

I felt like I had a basic understanding of the concept of rending the heart. I had had an experience with the Lord in Argentina where He had said to me concerning a place, "If you will rend your heart, I will rend the heaven." I knew that Evan

Roberts had prayed Isaiah 64:1 as one of the key Scriptural prayers of the Welsh revival. *"Oh that thou wouldest rend the heavens, that thou wouldest come down, that the mountains might flow down at thy presence"* (KJV). It is this concept of God tearing open the heavens that is linked so strongly to major revival and to city transformation.

For those not familiar with the concept of *rending* as it is used in Scripture, please walk with me through a brief teaching on it. The word for *rend* that appears in Joel 2:13 and in Isaiah 64:1 appears 63 times in the Bible. Most frequently, according to the *Theological Wordbook of the Old Testament*, it refers to an act of heartfelt and grievous affliction. In 36 of those appearances it is linked to rending or tearing the clothes as an outward sign of grief, mourning, repentance, humility, etc.

In Joshua 7:6 we read, *"And Joshua rent his clothes, and fell to the earth upon his face before the ark of the LORD until the eventide, he and the elders of Israel, and put dust upon their heads"* (KJV).

Joshua is mourning and expressing his distress over the defeat of the armies of Israel at the city of Ai. May I suggest when the nation is being defeated, it is time to fall on our face before God, and let our hearts be torn before Him. When the church is not victorious over the forces of darkness, it is time for us in the church to fall on our faces before God in repentance, weeping, etc.

It appears again in 1 Kings 21:27, *"And it came to pass, when Ahab heard those words, that he rent his clothes, and put sackcloth upon his flesh, and fasted, and lay in sackcloth, and went softly"* (KJV). I find this to be such an encouraging verse.

When Ahab repents and humbles himself before God, God responds to this king who has become a symbol, along with Jezebel, his wife, for almost everything that is wicked. Listen to God's response, *"And the word of the LORD came to Elijah the Tishbite, saying, Seest thou how Ahab humbleth himself before me? Because he humbleth himself before me, I will not bring the evil in his days: but in his son's days will I bring the evil upon his house"* (1 Kings 21:28-29 — KJV).

How much more will God respond to His people if we, too, would rend our hearts?

In the story of King Josiah, this rending is mentioned twice. First, we read in 2 Kings 22:11 *"And it came to pass, when the king had heard the words of the book of the law, that he rent his clothes."* (KJV). As King Josiah heard the Word of God and became aware of how they had violated it, he expressed his repentance and grief over their sin with the rending of his clothes.

In response, the prophetess Huldah declares the Word of the LORD to Josiah, *"Because thine heart was tender, and thou hast humbled thyself before the LORD, when thou heardest what I spake against this place, and against the inhabitants thereof, that they should become a desolation and a curse, and hast rent thy clothes, and wept before me; I also have heard thee, saith the LORD"* (2Kings 22:19 - KJV). This rending contributed to the national revival that followed in Josiah's day.

Rending occurs again in Ezra 9:3-5 when Ezra becomes aware of the sins of the people, he begins to rend his clothes over his anguish at their sin. *"And when I heard this thing, I rent my garment and my mantle, and plucked off the hair of my head and of my beard, and sat down astonied. Then were assembled unto me every one that trembled at the words of the God of Israel, because of the transgression of those that had been carried away; and I sat astonied until the evening sacrifice. And at the evening sacrifice I arose up from my heaviness; and having rent my garment and my mantle, I fell upon my knees, and spread out my hands unto the LORD my God"* (KJV).

Eight or nine verses (depending how you count them) link rending with the tearing of a Kingdom away from one person and giving it to another. Usually, this occurred because of sin and disobedience in the life of the one losing the Kingdom. It is not unfair to say because they would not rend their hearts, God rent their Kingdom from them.

If I understand the flow of the usage of rending, then in terms of it being related to repentance, grieving, mourning, humility, etc., then it seems to me the thrust of the word I felt came from the Lord for me to share with New Zealand was a call to repentance.

In our text I notice the following related concepts.

There was to be a turning to the Lord with all of the heart. Turning to the Lord of necessity has always involved the turning away from sin. This is not to be a halfway measure. Rather, it is to be with all of our hearts.

It involved fasting. It involved weeping. It involved mourning. John Calvin says this was wailing. This is being so moved by the situation that we respond beyond our cultural and religious boundaries.

I am not issuing a call for emotionalism, but I am saying this must reach the very deep of our being. At the risk of being offensive to Kiwis (New Zealanders), when we are more deeply moved over the loss of a rugby game than the sin of a nation, our priorities are out of focus. When it is proper to weep at a movie but wrong to weep in God's House, something is wrong.

In Jeremiah 4:30 God challenges a people who were ready to rend their face to secure the help of Egypt, but would not rend their hearts to secure the help of God. *"And when thou art spoiled, what wilt thou do? Though thou clothest thyself with crimson, though thou deckest thee with ornaments of gold, though thou rentest thy face with painting, in vain shalt thou make thyself fair; thy lovers will despise thee, they will seek thy life"* (KJV).

This fourth chapter describes the coming invasion by the Babylonians. The situation calls for the people of God to return to the Lord, but instead, they are described in verse thirty as a woman trying to make herself more attractive for a lover. Some see it like a prostitute preparing to go to the street. *"Thou rentest thy face with painting"* is translated in the NIV and other translations as *"Why shade your eyes with paint?"*

In fact let me share the NIV on this verse, *"What are you doing, O devastated one? Why dress yourself in scarlet and put on jewels of gold? Why shade your eyes with paint? You adorn yourself in vain. Your lovers despise you; they seek your life."*

Could it be that, often, when the time has grown desperate, the church has dressed itself for getting the attention of Egypt rather than rending its heart before the Lord? The programs of flesh have not transformed our cities. Is it not time for us to seek the Lord?

The passage in Joel involved the rending of the heart, not the garments. This was not to be an outward, religious show of repentance only. Oh yes, in this second chapter a call would go forth for national fasting and repentance. They were to:

Blow the trumpet in Zion,

sanctify a fast,

call a solemn assembly.

Gather the people,

sanctify the congregation, including the elders, the children, and the babies (those that suckled the breast).

Honeymoons were to be delayed, for the bridegroom was to *"go forth of his chamber, and the bride out of her closet"* (KJV).

The spiritual leadership was to be summoned, *"Let the priests, the ministers of the LORD… come and lead the way in weeping between the porch and the altar"* (KJV).

They were to call out to God for His mercy and intervention.

All this was to be done with the hope that the rending of the heart would cause God to rend the heavens and maybe— *"he will return and repent, and leave a blessing behind"* (KJV).

I am further challenged by a word to the Prophet Hosea in Hosea 13:8, *"I will meet them as a bear that is bereaved of her whelps, and will rend the caul of their heart, and there will I devour them like a lion: the wild beast shall tear them"* (KJV). As a part of the coming judgment on a sinful people, the prophet describes the actions of the Lord as being like a lion, a leopard, and a bear. The part that directly relates to us is the bear. In one sense the use of the three wild animals is probably a visual of the extremities of the judgment that is coming. Yet, notice the specific thing the bear will do. It will *"rend the caul of their heart."* Or as the NAS declares, *"I will tear open their chests."* The sense seems to be that since the people of God would not turn from their sins and since

94

they would not rend their hearts, then God Himself would cause their hearts to be rent open in His judgment on them.

We can celebrate the goodness of what God has and is doing among us — I would not want to take that away — we need those moments. [remember, I was preaching this in a corporate service of celebration.] Yet, I would call the church of New Zealand to do two things.

Own your own revival — let it get into your heart.

Rend your own heart — so He can return and bring a blessing.

I bring this message, to completion with the Scripture found in Ecclesiastes 3:7, *"A time to rend, and a time to sew; a time to keep silence, and a time to speak"* (KJV). I have always read this verse as a beautiful expression of poetry describing the seasons in our lives.

I was stunned to read John Gill's remarks on this verse. Gill links the time to rend with the times in the life of the church (Israel) where repentance and mourning was called for. The time to sew, he links to the times of sewing together the garments that had been rent during the repentance. In other words, when the repentance had been complete...when the revival had broken forth then it was time to sew — the weeping was over — the time to laugh had come.

The longer I worked on this message, the more hesitant I was to share it. I did not want to be out of the flow of an evening of celebration. I did not want to be a damper on what should be a great night of rejoicing at the goodness of God. At the same time, we cannot stop a race if we have not crossed the finish line.

I am going to call the church of New Zealand to examine its heart before God. I am not seeking to put a guilt trip on anyone. I am seeking to bring a Word from the heart of God to us.

Will you take ownership of a move of God in your nation?

Spiritual leaders, will you move beyond your own kingdom and build His?

People of the church of New Zealand — will you allow the vision of your pastors to become your vision? Will you make church more than just a Sunday thing? Will you want revival so bad you can taste it? Are you willing to be despised if that is what it takes? Will you rend your hearts...and not your garments...before the Lord until He rends open the heavens?

This message is complete, but how do we respond to it?

May I suggest some of us will need to ask the Lord, "How do I take ownership of revival in my area?" For some of us, it will start with a fresh burden to impact our neighborhood... school...place of work, and so forth. The Lord will begin to show you some creative ways you can share His message. You are going to sense you are God's answer to your situation. There are opportunities present before us.

I am going to ask us to rend our hearts...to come before the Lord with repentance for our own lives...our own lack of passion for revival...our apathy over the sins of the church and city.

Would you consider giving a day per week or perhaps a day per month to fast and pray for revival in your church, city, nation?

The largest single salvation response to the message in this chapter was 250 people in a conference in Roxas City, Philippines.

Luke 4:18-19, "The Spirit of the Lord is upon me, because he hath anointed me to preach the gospel to the poor; he hath sent me to heal the brokenhearted, to preach deliverance to the captives, and recovering of sight to the blind, to set at liberty them that are bruised, To preach the acceptable year of the Lord." – KJV

Luke 4:18-19, "The Spirit of the Lord is on me, because he has anointed me to preach good news to the poor. He has sent me to proclaim freedom for the prisoners and recovery of sight for the blind, to release the oppressed, to proclaim the year of the Lord's favour." – NIV

CHAPTER TEN

ANOINTED FOR THREE THINGS

The message in this chapter is going to be a simple message. It is a message full of hope and good news. If I were speaking in a public setting, I would say this message is about Someone who is in this place today and what He wants to do in your life. So let me say this to my readers. This message is about Someone who is with you as you are reading this chapter.

At the close of this chapter I am going to be giving you an opportunity to respond to the Lord. Some are going to respond to an opportunity of getting your sins forgiven. Some are going to respond to an opportunity of receiving healing in your life. Still others are going to respond to an opportunity of experiencing a freedom and victory in your life that you desperately need.

If I was preaching this to you in person, I would be asking the Lord to release a special anointing in the place where the meeting

97

is being held. So I am asking the Lord, even as I write this, to release a special anointing as you read what I have written.

I have three simple points I want to emphasize in this chapter. However, before sharing them, I want to deal with another truth. Jesus said, *"The Spirit of the Lord is upon me, because he hath anointed me"* (KJV). In the final analysis, Jesus is the anointed One. We may experience levels of His anointing resting on us — and flowing through us — but Jesus is the Anointed One. We can serve as channels, but He is the reservoir — the source.

Therefore, if Jesus is the Anointed One, I want you to look to Him today. I want you to look beyond the writer to what is written. I am grateful to the Lord for the anointing that rests upon me as I pray for someone, but it is so important we look beyond the vessel who prays for us and look to the One who answers prayer. I never forget that which will bring healing, salvation, and freedom is that which comes from the Spirit of the LORD. I dare not presume that I am the source. I can, and must, move out in faith in the anointing of the Holy Spirit, but it is He who is the Anointed One.

I am not going to do an in depth teaching on the anointing in this chapter, but I want to observe two things. The anointing has to do with being set aside for a purpose and then being equipped to fulfill that purpose.

With that in mind, what was Jesus anointed to do? What was He set aside to do and equipped to do? For this is the very thing He will do today in your life as you come to Him.

The Anointing Is To Bring Salvation

Jesus was anointed to preach. Three times He states that fact in two verses, which suggests to me that preaching is important. He said He was anointed *"to preach the gospel"* or as the NIV says, *"preach good news."* Then He said He was anointed *"to preach deliverance"* or to *"proclaim freedom"* according to the NIV. Finally, He said He was anointed *"To preach the acceptable year"* or *"to proclaim the year of the Lord's favour"* (NIV).

In making these declarations, Jesus actually uses two different Greek words. One word focuses on the content. It is translated *"to preach the gospel."* Its focus is on the message — which is a message of good news. Friend, I bring good news today.

The good news is that everyone reading this book was born a sinner. This sin will take you to hell. However, God loves you and has a plan for your life. He does not want you to go to hell. He wants you to come and live with Him forever in a place called heaven that He has prepared just for you. Jesus died so that plan of bringing you to heaven could work for you. If you ask Jesus to forgive you and to come into your life, you can be forgiven of your sins. Your faith in what He did activates what He has done for you.

That is the bare bones of this good news.

The other word focuses on the authority of the One speaking. It is authority because you are speaking on behalf of One who has all power. The same word is used to describe a herald who is proclaiming a message on the behalf of a King. Friend, I am sharing on behalf of a King today. He has given me authority to tell you that your sins can be forgiven. I am not preaching fiction. He has given me authority to speak to you on His behalf.

This anointing to preach, first of all, is focused on salvation. This is the greatest news in the world. You and I can be forgiven for all our sins — there is a place where you can begin again, or have a start over. Sometimes when I was playing a game as a kid, I would ask for a "do over." In golf, we call it a mulligan. The past is wiped out, and we have a fresh start. Literally, the gospel gives us that opportunity. The language of Scripture calls it being born again. God wipes out the record of my past, and I get to start over, to have a "do over."

At the end of this message…at the end of this chapter, I want you to have a "do over" moment. You can make the decision to start over again. He wants you to do that. I want you to do that.

The Anointing Is To Bring Healing

Not only does the anointing bring salvation, but it is also for healing. First of all, there is healing for our physical needs. He came to bring sight to those who were blind. It is a tragedy when that which God intended for good has become so controversial. Healing was never intended to become a focus for debate. God intended it to be a blessing.

Every healing is an expression of four things. It is an expression of the love and compassion of God. Throughout the Gospels, the compassion of Jesus found expression in the healing of the sick. The summary is found in Matthew 14:14, *"And Jesus went forth, and saw a great multitude, and was moved with compassion toward them, and he healed their sick"* (KJV).

Every healing is an expression of the ultimate victory over death that we will experience. We understand that every one of us has an appointment with death. Every sickness reminds us of our frailty, but every healing reminds us that after death there is life. Sickness will ultimately be overcome.

Healing is an advance statement concerning the final defeat of Satan. The sin he introduced led to sickness and death. However, every healing reminds us that the destroyer will be destroyed.

Finally, healing reminds us of the faithfulness of God in keeping His Word.

Candidly, I do not have all of the answers to the healing questions. Why can I pray for one standing in an aisle, but the one sitting in the seat gets healed instead? I have prayed for those on their death beds, and funerals had to be delayed. I have prayed for others without any apparent success. To be honest, the questions are more than we can count, but I know I have been given permission to pray for the sick. Indeed, I have been given authority to do so.

I prayed with a man we will call "Jack," on a Sunday morning. He was going into the hospital for heart surgery the following morning. Blockages needed to be removed. Before the procedure a final set of X-rays were taken. Jack was lying on the gurney quietly singing a song that had a line that says, "He healed my body." As the doctor was placing the X-rays on the viewing screen, he asked Jack what he was singing. Jack said, "Oh, just a little song we sing at church." In a few moments the doctor excitedly grabbed the X-rays and ran into the hall. Jack could hear him say, "Look at these X-rays. Where did the blockages go? This man's blood is flowing like a river." Yes, He still heals our bodies.

A staff pastor in Missouri sent me this story, "When you were at our church, you prayed for a woman that had a cyst on her brain... she went back to the doctor and guess what?... OH YEAH, YOU GUESSED IT, GOD HEALED HER!!!!!!!! That's what He does, that's who He is, that's my Savior!!!"

Not only does He heal our physical needs, but there is also healing for our emotional needs. You see, He came to heal the brokenhearted. One preacher asked God to show him how He saw the world. The next thing that happened was, he suddenly saw a vision of the world with a broken heart.

From early in life we begin to experience disappointments. Devastating things are said to us. Unspeakably bad things happen to us. Our emotions are often more tattered than our bodies. But today you can bring the hurts of your life to the Cross. The anointing heals those who are heartbroken.

The Anointing Is To Set People Free

Not only does the anointing bring salvation and healing, but it also brings freedom. Strongholds keep many from experiencing the freedom God intends for them to have. Notice two things Jesus says in our text. He came to *"proclaim deliverance to the captive"* (KJV). He came to proclaim freedom for you. Secondly, He came to set bruised ones free. The NIV says *"to release the oppressed."*

Some strongholds relate to habits that keep people in bondage. A deacon described to me a ten-year battle with the habit of smoking. He was convinced God wanted him free from this habit that would probably bring sickness into his life. And that freedom came!

Some strongholds have to do with demonic activity. During his earthly ministry, Jesus not only healed people, but He also set people free from demonic bondage.

Some deliverance is instantaneous. I am thinking of the lady in a revival in New Zealand who was saved and delivered from smoking in the same moment. Or, I could tell about a drug dealer who found Jesus not only as his Saviour, but who was also the Deliverer from twenty-plus years of pot and heroin.

Some deliverances from demonic activity are very dramatic and instantaneous. I was asked to go to the rear of a building in Ecuador where a missionary was dealing with a man who was clearly experiencing demonic activity. I slipped into the secondary role as the missionary continued to bind the activity of the demon. After a few minutes, the bondage of the demon was broken, and the man was set free.

I chose this story because it has a humorous subplot. During the deliverance session, the man had attempted to spit on me and to hit me with his Bible. Once the man was free, the missionary turned to me and said, "That demon did not like you." I responded, "It was mutual. I did not like it, either." As soon as I had walked up to the demonized man, I knew instantly I had dealt with this demon before. I do not know how I knew, but I knew I had removed this demon, through the power of Jesus' name, from another person. And the demon recognized me. It knew that I knew it was going to go. And it did. I prefer that type of deliverance.

But some deliverance may be progressive. On the third night of special meetings, I heard myself say to a person, "You are accepted in the Beloved." That simple Biblical statement set off an entirely unexpected reaction. One did not need to be a spiritual genius to recognize the demonic manifestation. I was to learn later this person had been sexually abused from childhood. The chief perpetrator would say, "You are not accepted by God." That, of course, was a lie. She was accepted. The deliverance and healing she received was a journey. Over a number of ministry situations, demonic activity would be dealt with, and healing for the brokenness would come. I asked the Lord, "Why was this breakthrough progressive rather than instantaneous?" I felt like He said that because He understood the person was so fragile, an instantaneous deliverance and healing would have actually brought even greater damage. So, He would heal and set free at a pace that could be handled. I prefer instantaneous. He prefers complete!

As I bring this chapter to a close and before I give you an opportunity to respond to the One who sent me to be a proclaimer, I want you to observe one final thing.

Jesus came to preach the acceptable year of the Lord. May I say to you this is an accepted time? Scripture says now is the time of salvation. Jesus sees one bound by disease and asks him if he is ready to be healed. The man was waiting for an angel to stir the water at the pool of Bethesda, but One greater than an angel had come, and it was a time acceptable for healing. There is a time to be set free. Why not go for it?

Another way to translate acceptable year is the year of favor or the time of favor. This is a time of God's favor. You can enter into that favor today.

The *Amplified* version of our text says: "*To proclaim the accepted and acceptable year of the Lord [the day] when salvation and the free favors of God profusely abound.*" The Luke 4:19 passage is a quote from Isaiah 61:1-2 which reads: "*The Spirit of the Lord GOD is upon me; because the LORD hath anointed me to preach good tidings unto the meek; he hath sent me to bind up the brokenhearted, to proclaim liberty to the captives, and the opening of the prison to them that are bound; To proclaim the acceptable year of the LORD, and the day of vengeance of our God; to comfort all that mourn*" (KJV).

It is a promise of national restoration for Judah, but it is also a Messianic passage, a reference to Jesus. Jesus actually stops reading the passage in the middle of what we call verse two, but I want you to see the following truth. Jesus stops, because He has read as far as He needs to read. He says "I am the fulfillment of this verse." This is just one of many passages where Jesus claims to be the Messiah.

Notice most of His ministry was to be what we would call positive. According to our text, He would *"preach good tidings… bind up brokenhearted…proclaim liberty…opening of the prison… comfort all that mourn…beauty for ashes…joy for mourning…praise for the spirit of heaviness…trees of righteousness"* (KJV). WHAT A GLORIOUS AND WONDERFUL EXCHANGE! But the Isaiah passage also has a negative side — *"the day of vengeance of our God."* As the Messiah in His earthly ministry, Jesus would bring healing, deliverance, and salvation, but as the Messiah in His judicial ministry, He will release *"the day of vengeance of our God."* I must stress that every use of the word vengeance, and its root word, are negative. His judicial ministry will not be pleasant to His enemies.

Wrath or mercy! It is your choice.

The *Amplified* describes this day of acceptance as *"the day when salvation and the free favors of God profusely abound."* I want to suggest there are days or seasons of special grace and outpourings from God's Spirit. There are days when salvations abound — when it seems easy for people to get saved. In a 15-week meeting in Michigan City, Indiana, the pastor observed we were seeing weekly the type of salvations that often only occurred once a generation in a church. During that revival I think I could have read Matthew 1 and given a salvation altar call — and people would have gotten saved. While the logos of God's Word was always available, it seemed the rhema of God's Word had come.

First Peter 2:12 describes a day of visitation where God would be glorified. Some scholars believe this passage refers to the day of end time judgment, while others believe this is a reference to seasons of gracious outpourings of God's Spirit — times where God comes near to evaluate and minister to His people.

Revivals are these sort of times, but tragically, these seasons can be missed. Jesus speaks of Jerusalem as knowing not *"the time of their visitation."* This may refer to the coming judgment of God, but more likely, He was the visitation being sent by God (Luke 19:44) and they were about to miss who He was.

A visitation from God must be recognized and entered into during the season of the visitation. There was a time to cross the Jordan and enter the promised land — later would not work. Scripture describes those who had missed salvation's time and would cry out for entrance only to be denied (Luke 13:25). Isaiah 55:6 exhorts us to *"seek the Lord while he may be found, call…upon him while he is near"* (KJV).

I believe this is a great opportunity for those who need to be forgiven of sins to ask Jesus to become their Saviour.

I believe this is a great opportunity for those in need of healing of body and soul to call out to Him.

The third opportunity is for those who are struggling in an area of your life, and you would like to ask Jesus to set you free.

Finally, this is an opportunity to seek for the increase of anointing on your life, so you can minister more effectively to others.

Feel free to pray this prayer with me.

"Jesus, I admit I have sinned. I want to repent, that is, I want to turn away from my sin. Jesus, I want to ask You to forgive me for my sin. I have hurt You. I have hurt others. I have hurt myself. I am sorry. I ask You to forgive me. I believe You are the Son of God. I believe You came to this earth from heaven. I believe You were born of a virgin birth. I invite You into my life. I ask You to wash away my sin with Your blood. I believe that You said in John 1:12 if I would receive You I would become a child of God. I receive you now."

If you have prayed that prayer and surrendered your life to Jesus, I would love to hear about it. You can email me at mikliven@aol.com, or go to mikelivengoodministries.com and share your story there by going to the contact page.

Now let me pray with you for healing of body and soul. "Father, I pray for the reader of this book. I remind You that You declared your word can be sent and healing comes. I now lift before You my friend who is on the other side of this page. I ask that You release the healing for them that Your Son purchased at the Cross. In the Name of Jesus, I take authority over the sickness now being experienced by my friend. I command that sickness to go because He gives me authority to speak His Word. In the Name of Jesus, be healed in body and soul."

And now, Father, I pray for freedom to be given to my readers. It is not Your will they be subject to oppression and bondage. You came to set the prisoner free. In the Name of Jesus, I release freedom in your life. I release freedom from habits. I also release freedom from demonic spirits that have controlled my friend. Spirits, I remind you that whom the Son sets free is free indeed so I command you to set them free from your control now.

Finally, even as You filled and re-filled Your church in Acts with Your Spirit bringing a fresh anointing, I ask You to fill every hungry reader of this chapter with Your Spirit. Let the anointing increase, I ask in the Name of Jesus!"

While much of the focus of revival is on the lost coming to Jesus, revival also deals with living in a very real world. Revival will be opposed by Satan. While I prefer not to give him much ink, spiritual war creates casualties.

This message is to help people understand what is happening and how to overcome.

CHAPTER ELEVEN

WAR ON THE SAINTS

The dreams and visions of Daniel have great significance for us today. One of those visions comes in Daniel 7. The first fourteen verses of this chapter describe this dream.

"In the first year of Belshazzar king of Babylon Daniel had a dream and visions of his head upon his bed: then he wrote the dream, and told the sum of the matters. Daniel spake and said, I saw in my vision by night, and, behold, the four winds of the heaven strove upon the great sea. And four great beasts came up from the sea, diverse one from another. The first was like a lion, and had eagle's wings: I beheld till the wings thereof were plucked, and it was lifted up from the earth, and made stand upon the feet as a man, and a man's heart was given to it. And behold another beast, a second, like to a bear, and it raised up itself on one side, and it had three ribs in the mouth of it between the teeth of it: and they said thus unto it, Arise, devour much flesh. After this I beheld, and lo another, like a leopard, which had upon the back of it four wings of a fowl; the beast had also four heads; and dominion was given to it. After this I saw in the night visions, and behold a fourth beast, dreadful and terrible, and strong exceedingly; and it had great iron teeth: it devoured and brake in pieces, and stamped the residue

with the feet of it: and it was diverse from all the beasts that were before it; and it had ten horns. I considered the horns, and, behold, there came up among them another little horn, before whom there were three of the first horns plucked up by the roots: and, behold, in this horn were eyes like the eyes of man, and a mouth speaking great things.

I beheld till the thrones were cast down, and the Ancient of days did sit, whose garment was white as snow, and the hair of his head like the pure wool: his throne was like the fiery flame, and his wheels as burning fire. A fiery stream issued and came forth from before him: thousand thousands ministered unto him, and ten thousand times ten thousand stood before him: the judgment was set, and the books were opened. I beheld then because of the voice of the great words which the horn spake: I beheld even till the beast was slain, and his body destroyed, and given to the burning flame. As concerning the rest of the beasts, they had their dominion taken away: yet their lives were prolonged for a season and time. I saw in the night visions, and, behold, one like the Son of man came with the clouds of heaven, and came to the Ancient of days, and they brought him near before him. And there was given him dominion, and glory, and a kingdom, that all people, nations, and languages, should serve him: his dominion is an everlasting dominion, which shall not pass away, and his kingdom that which shall not be destroyed."

Let me summarize those fourteen verses. Verses 1-8 describe four beasts that arise from the sea. The description of those terrifying and mystifying beasts is followed by a vision of the Ancient of Days in verses 9-14. He is described in verse 9. In verse 10 He is worshipped, and judgment is set. Verses 11-12 describe the destruction of the beasts, and in verses 13-14 the Son of Man is given an eternal kingdom.

The balance of the chapter is given to interpreting the dream.

"I Daniel was grieved in my spirit in the midst of my body, and the visions of my head troubled me. I came near unto one of them that stood by, and asked him the truth of all this. So he told me, and made me know the interpretation of the things. These great beasts, which are four, are four kings, which shall arise out of the earth. But the saints

of the most High shall take the kingdom, and possess the kingdom for ever, even for ever and ever. Then I would know the truth of the fourth beast, which was diverse from all the others, exceeding dreadful, whose teeth were of iron, and his nails of brass; which devoured, brake in pieces, and stamped the residue with his feet; And of the ten horns that were in his head, and of the other which came up, and before whom three fell; even of that horn that had eyes, and a mouth that spake very great things, whose look was more stout than his fellows. I beheld, and the same horn made war with the saints, and prevailed against them; Until the Ancient of days came, and judgment was given to the saints of the most High; and the time came that the saints possessed the kingdom. Thus he said, The fourth beast shall be the fourth kingdom upon earth, which shall be diverse from all kingdoms, and shall devour the whole earth, and shall tread it down, and break it in pieces. And the ten horns out of this kingdom are ten kings that shall arise: and another shall rise after them; and he shall be diverse from the first, and he shall subdue three kings. And he shall speak great words against the most High, and shall wear out the saints of the most High, and think to change times and laws: and they shall be given into his hand until a time and times and the dividing of time. But the judgment shall sit, and they shall take away his dominion, to consume and to destroy it unto the end. And the kingdom and dominion, and the greatness of the kingdom under the whole heaven, shall be given to the people of the saints of the most High, whose kingdom is an everlasting kingdom, and all dominions shall serve and obey him. Hitherto is the end of the matter. As for me Daniel, my cogitations much troubled me, and my countenance changed in me: but I kept the matter in my heart" (KJV).

This vision brings a *"grieving"* in Daniel's spirit, and it *"troubled"* his head. He was greatly impacted by what he had seen. Daniel inquires of the angel, who is a part of his dream, as to the meaning of what he has just seen. The summary of the vision is given in Daniel 7:16-18. In verses 16-17 four kingdoms shall arise out of the earth, but in verse 18 the saints shall *"take"* and *"possess"* the Kingdom *"forever."*

Daniel is still disturbed and wants to understand the fourth beast, which is described again in verses 19-20 as *"diverse... exceeding dreadful."* It is described as one who *"devours"* and *"stomps"* and is *"more stout"* than the others. Daniel 7:21 describes the fourth beast's relationship to the saints in two statements. *"He makes war with the saints"* and *"prevailed against them."* This situation remains until in verse 22, the Ancient of Days intervenes, then judgment is given to the saints. This judgment is a judicial decision in their favor, which leads to the saints taking possession of the Kingdom.

The angel goes on to give a fuller explanation regarding the fourth beast in verses 23-27. We are given in verses 23-24 the nature and extent of the fourth beast. His is a fourth Kingdom. *It is diverse...he devours...he treads...he breaks in pieces.* We are given a picture of part of this kingdom subduing three others. Verse 25 describes an attack against the saints. First, the beast speaks *"great words against the most High."* The beast plans to *"wear out the saints of the most High."* Third, the beast thinks to *"change times and laws."* He will be successful in doing this for three and one-half years.

However in Daniel 7:26-27, the situation changes and the victory of the saints is assured. The *"judgment shall sit"* against the beast. His dominion is *"taken away...consumed...destroyed."* After this the Kingdom will be given to the saints. This Kingdom will be *"an everlasting Kingdom and all dominions shall serve and obey Him."*

Please notice in verse 28 Daniel's response. He kept the matter in his heart. However, his countenance is changed and the KJV says his *"cogitations much troubled him."*

What is the message I believe I am to share with you?

I am not going into the prophetic meaning of the passage any further than we have gone, although that would be a needed subject. I want to speak into the area of spiritual warfare, because some of you are experiencing, or will experience Satanic attack against you. This will increase in the days you are entering.

110

I believe Satan has strategies he uses and in this picture of his last days' attack against the saints, we see the strategies he will use against you today. I have a three-point message for you. We will focus on the following:

THE WAR ON THE SAINTS
THE FUTURE OF THE SAINTS
THE FAITH OF THE SAINTS.

Let us begin with Satan's war on the saints.

The War on the Saints

Let us be clear on this, Satan is at war with you. Daniel 7:21 is the only time this specific Hebrew word for war appears in the KJV. It comes from a word that appears nine times. Those nine appearances are translated battle five times and war four times. While a couple of those usages can be described as spiritual warfare, most of the verses are strongly literal. I believe the end time war will be physical, but at present it is largely emotional, mental, and spiritual for most of God's people. The root word, which appears 280 times in diverse usages, literally means *"to approach ... for whatever purpose."* As the root for the word *war*, I assume the connection is the face-to-face nature of battle in that day.

In Psalm 55:18,21, David describes God delivering his soul in peace from the battle and describes an enemy with smooth-as-butter words, but war in his heart.

Psalm 55:18,21, *"He hath delivered my soul in peace from the battle that was against me: for there were many with me....The words of his mouth were smoother than butter, but war was in his heart: his words were softer than oil, yet were they drawn swords"*(KJV).

What a graphic picture of Satan! His words are often smoother than butter. He can make it sound good, but do not be deceived. He has war in his heart toward you. His words may appear soft, but he has drawn his sword.

Daniel's dream not only portrayed a battle with Satan, but Satan was actually prevailing against the saints. Often, he still appears to be winning the battle.

While the word *prevail* is used by most translators, other words are used. One major translation uses the word *overpowering*. Another uses the word *defeating*. Yet another optional translation is *overcame*. The adversary was attacking or warring against the saints of God and appeared to be succeeding in his endeavor until, in verse 22, the Ancient of Days came. Victory over Satan comes here because of Divine intervention.

This is where some of you are living right now. You are struggling for spiritual survival. You feel like you are about to go under spiritually. Some of you are overwhelmed, not so much in your personal circumstances, but you see the advance of darkness and the attack on your belief system, and you feel your defenses crumbling. Social media discussions, governmental decisions, and statistics suggesting Christianity is losing ground have caused you to feel like Jesus is losing.

In verse 25 Satan wears out the saints. *Brown-Driver-Briggs Lexicon* says the word means to wear away or to wear out and is used "to harass constantly…and is (used only in a mental sense)."

Strong's Concordance agrees that the use of this word is "in a mental sense" and literally, it is "to afflict". It is translated "wear out." It is also translated *wear down* (NAS95), *oppress* (NIV), *persecute* (NKJV), *crush* (DRV) *attempting to put an end to the saints* (BBE).

Satan's primary strategy against you is going to be a constant battle on your mind, the purpose of which is to bring you to a place of being worn out or exhausted spiritually to where you feel like you do not have the strength to continue. He will try to wear you out two ways.

First, he *"shall speak great words against the most high"* (7:25). Four times the NKJV uses the expression *"pompous words"* (7:8, 11, 20, 25). Three times these words are a general description of the language of one probably identified as the anti-christ. Once it is used to describe the exact words he speaks against the Most High God.

Have you noticed how blatant and offensive the language is becoming against believers, the church, and even against the Most

High God Himself? Some of you are living in work environments, educational situations, homes, or neighborhoods where you and what you believe are under a constant attack, verbally.

Second, he *"shall intend to change times and laws"* (7:25). Satan is attempting to re-define what is good and evil. He is attempting to do away with God's laws regarding sin and write his own laws. Today, if you hold to Biblical standards regarding sexual morality, you are not just antiquated, but you are intolerant. Even as I write this, the downward plunge of multiple societies increases at a rapid pace. Good and evil are no longer defined by the interpretations God has given them. Today, gender identity appears to be the whim of the moment. Biological definition of gender has now been replaced by emotional definition. The fixed *"times and laws"* from antiquity have been replaced by transitory *"laws."*

Satan is also redefining God's requirements for entrance into heaven. Pluralism, which is the teaching that many roads can take you to heaven, and Universalism, which teaches everybody goes to heaven, are but two expressions of this.

Psalm 78 speaks eloquently to this mindset, so we will examine a few applicable verses and phrases in verses 5-16 of the NKJV, *"For He established a testimony in Jacob, and appointed a law in Israel, which He commanded our fathers, that they should make them known to their children; that the generation to come might know them, the children who would be born, that they may arise and declare them to their children, that they may set their hope in God, and not forget the works of God, but keep His commandments; and may not be like their fathers, a stubborn and rebellious generation, a generation that did not set its heart aright, and whose spirit was not faithful to God. The Children of Ephraim, being armed and carrying bows, turned back in the day of battle. They did not keep the covenant of God; they refused to walk in His law, and forgot His works and His wonders that He had shown them. Marvelous things He did in the sight of their fathers, in the land of Egypt, in the field of Zoan. He divided the sea and caused them to pass through; and He made the waters stand up like a heap. In the daytime also He led them with the cloud, and all the night with a light of fire. He split the rocks in the wilderness, and gave them drink in abundance like the depths. He also brought streams out of the rock, And caused waters to run down like rivers."*

God had revealed His Word…His testimonies…His commandments to His people. His people were to pass the Word of God on to the next generation. The fathers were to make them known to their children so that they could know the Lord. Then, that generation was to pass the Word of God on to the next generation so that they could *"set their hope in God."* They were not to *"forget the works of God."*

Not only had God given them His Word, but they had also seen His works and wonders, but they forgot what He had done in Egypt to deliver them. They forgot about the miracle at the Red Sea. They had forgotten the water that gushed out of the rock in the desert.

The first generation had become stubborn and rebellious. They had not set their heart in the right place. God had marvelously equipped them for the day of battle. They were armed and carrying bows, but they had turned back in the day of battle.

Psalm 78:17-19 continues the description, *"But they sinned even more against Him by rebelling against the Most High in the wilderness, and they tested God in their heart by asking for the food of their fancy. Yes, they spoke against God: they said, 'Can God prepare a table in the wilderness?'"* They sinned by rebellion. In verse 18 they tested God; in verse 19 they spoke against God and His provision.

In Psalm 78:22 *"they did not believe in God, and did not trust in His salvation."* Verse 32 reveals they persisted in sin for *"they still sinned, and did not believe in His wondrous works."*

In spite of the failure of these people, the record of the 78th Psalm is that for a long season, God continued to grace them. He continued to lead them in verse 14. He not only led them, but His Glory was present among them as a cloud by day and fire by night. He provided water in verses 15-16, in verses 24-25

He provided them of the bread of heaven, sending them food to the full.

Eventually, however, their rebellion brought God's wrath and judgment. I read in Psalm 78: 21,31, *"the LORD heard this and was furious; so a fire was kindled against Jacob, and anger also came up against Israel…The wrath of God came against them, and slew the stoutest of them, and struck down the choice men of Israel."*

We learn in Psalm 78:34 *"they returned and sought earnestly for God."* In others words, they came to a place of repentance. And He, according to verse 38, *"being full of compassion, forgave their iniquity."*

If our forefathers were correct in their understanding of prophetic Scripture, and I have no reason to disagree with their conclusions, we can expect opposition to increase. Persecution and suffering may well be in all of our futures. The world is not a friend of Jesus.

Psalms 78 reminds us the default position of the Lord God is to move toward people in compassion, but continued rebellion will eventually bring His judgment. Please turn to Him while His compassion is there.

Do not be surprised at the war on the saints.

The Future of the Saints

Is defeat the future of the saints of God? No, they *"possess the Kingdom forever"* (Daniel 7:18). Another translation says they *"take the Kingdom."* According to *Strong's* this is *"to acquire"* and is usually translated *receive* or *take*.

According to *B-D-B*, all three appearances of this word are in Daniel. In each case the word is used to describe something that is being received. In Daniel 2:6 the King tells the Chaldeans they will receive gifts from him if they can interpret the dream he has had. In Daniel 5:31 Darius the Mede receives the Kingdom at the death of Belshazzar. Here, it is forcible in that he attacked, but in 5:28 the prophetic word was Belshazzar's kingdom had been given to the Medes and Persians by God.

Therefore, it would seem clear to me the saints do not take or wrestle the Kingdom away from the four beasts, but God gives it to them. Our victory is as certain as the battle.

The saints will *"possess the Kingdom forever and forever"* (7:18). To possess is to hold in occupancy (*Strong's*). It is from a word implying *to hoard up*, and it only appears in Daniel 7:18,22. They will not be required to relinquish it. The Kingdom will belong to them. And they will *"receive it forever."*

Forever, according to *Strong's*, speaks literally of remote time, be it in the future or the past. It is not a place in time, but an indefinite. *B-D-B* says it is used for *perpetuity, antiquity, forever*. It is related to a word suggesting the vanishing point is concealed, and while it would not be required to always mean *forever*, it usually does. *B-D-B* says in reference to past, it is used to describe something from ancient time or long ago. In reference to future, it is used to describe *"forever, always; continuous existence, perpetual, everlasting, indefinite or unending future, eternity."* The root word literally means *"to veil from sight"*, i.e. *conceal*. It seems to me in relation to time, it is suggesting either the beginning, or the end, or both, cannot be seen; therefore, it speaks of eternity.

When the Ancient of Days comes in verse 22, then the fourth beast's kingdom, and all earthly kingdoms, surrender to the rulership, judgment or justice of the Ancient of Days. The saints possess the Kingdom because it is given to them by the Ancient of Days. Judgment was given to the saints of the most High. The scene is that of a courtroom, and the Eternal Judge, the Ancient of Days pronounces His forever verdict.

Other translations make this thought clear. The NAS 95 says, *"Judgment was passed in favor of the saints of the Highest One."* The NIV says *"and pronounced judgment in favor of the saints of the Most High."* The NKJV prefers *"judgment was made in favor of the saints,"* while the BBE uses, *"decision was made and the authority was given to the saints."*

In verse 27 the ultimate triumph is given to the saints. This which is given to the saints includes *"the kingdom and dominion, and the greatness of the kingdom under the whole heaven."* Secondly, the kingdom is given to the *"saints."* The word *saints* is not to be understood as a group of super spiritual people, but simply as those who have been born into His Kingdom. Thirdly, His Kingdom is *"everlasting and all dominions shall serve and obey him."*

The NAS 95 is really strong here, *"Then the sovereignty, the dominion and the greatness of all the Kingdoms under the whole heaven will be given to the people of the saints of the Highest One; His Kingdom will be an everlasting Kingdom, and all dominions will serve and obey Him."*

The Faith of the Saints

At the conclusion of the angel's response to Daniel, the angel declares, *"hitherto is the end of the matter."* In other words, this is the end of the angel's words and the interpretation of Daniel's vision and the answer to everything Daniel wanted to know. Indeed, this chapter has actually described the final end of everything related to the Kingdom of God — and we win! We must know this.

Even with this assurance from the angel, Daniel said my *"cogitations much troubled me."* Strong's says the Hebrew of *cogitations* speaks of mental conception.

Daniel was alarmed by what he had seen. His mind was being overwhelmed. Try these words on for size. Daniel is terrified...troubled...alarmed...dismayed. Some of you are there. Faith tells us our future is secure, but at the moment, you are overwhelmed in your thinking.

The word appears six times, and all in Daniel. Daniel 2:29-30 the thoughts seem to be first the dream Nebuchadnezzar had and then his thinking about them (2:26,28). In 4:19 the thoughts are clearly Daniel's thinking or understanding. In 5:6 Belshazzar's thoughts alarm him. This is connected with the writing on the wall. In verse 10 the queen encourages him not to let his thoughts alarm him.

117

Most of the battle is in the space between our ears and behind our eyes. It is in our minds.

Faith brings our minds into the reality of the Word of God. Faith does not deny the existence of problems. Daniel had seen some things that were terrifying. Faith comes from the Word of God. I know my circumstances are challenging, but my faith still rests in the One who knew my circumstances before they arrived.

Not only did Daniel's cogitations bother him, but his *"countenance was changed."* The word for countenance appears six times in Scripture and all in Daniel. Two times the word is used to describe the splendor of an inanimate object (Nebuchadnezzar's statue and his kingdom). The other four times it refers to the face growing pale (NAS 95) or countenance changing. Daniel has a physical and emotional reaction, as well as a mental reaction, to what he has seen. What Daniel has seen not only affected his thinking, it caused a physical reaction as well.

I am trying to communicate that this is real world stuff. As believers, we are still subject to human impact.

So what did Daniel do?

Daniel *"kept the matter"* in his heart. That is, he guarded the vision and its meaning in his mind and heart. He did not let it escape. He continued to meditate, reflect, and ponder the triumph that was his. Do not let God's Word escape from your thinking. Keep it in your heart.

So What?

What do I want you to know and do with this message?

First, for those who are in the midst of a strong mental battle, your tremendous mental, emotional, and spiritual battles are not unusual. You are normal. Indeed, the day in which we are living is thrusting many into the greatest mental battles of their lives.

I write these lines as the Delta COVID continues to create headlines and is being joined by the newly-discovered Omicron variant. Not only are there issues around the disease itself, but concerns about political, social, and Biblical implications are creating much mental stress for many, many people.

I believe the Ancient of Days is preparing to call court to order on behalf of the church, and the victory is about to be given to you. Your triumph is certain—do not allow the enemy to smooth talk you out of the reality that is yours. If we were in a service together, I would be giving you the opportunity of experiencing prayer ministry where we would ask the Ancient of Days to enforce a victory on your behalf and to cause faith and courage to come until complete victory is yours.

Second, is for those who have not surrendered your lives to the Lordship of Jesus. While I have written primarily to the church, there is an application for you. The day will come when the Ancient of Days, God Almighty, will call Heaven's court to session. Only those who have served Him here will be given the right to enter Heaven and to rule with Him forever. I want you to be a part of that great day...that great Kingdom.

However, you cannot make the decision to live for Jesus after death or on the day of Judgment. That decision must be made today.

Will you make that decision today?

I am a Holy Ghost preacher. I believe strongly in the work of the Spirit. During the first twelve years of itinerant ministry, I would normally preach at least once per week on the Holy Spirit and pray specifically for people to receive the baptism in the Holy Spirit. During some of the extended meetings, I did not preach as often on the Holy Spirit. The leading of the Spirit and the flow of those meetings kept most of the preaching on salvation, sanctification, and Presence. We discovered that in the atmosphere of revival, many churches found that it was easy for people to be filled with the Spirit. When people were seeking for "more of the Lord," His response was often to fill them with His Spirit. This chapter is one of my favorite messages on the Spirit.

CHAPTER TWELVE

THE MINISTRY OF THE HOLY SPIRIT

ROMANS 15:13,16,19,30 — *"Now the God of hope fill you with all joy and peace in believing, that ye may abound in hope, through the power of the Holy Ghost...That I should be the minister of Jesus Christ to the Gentiles, ministering the gospel of God, that the offering up of the Gentiles might be acceptable, being sanctified by the Holy Ghost...Through mighty signs and wonders, by the power of the Spirit of God; so that from Jerusalem, and round about unto Illyricum, I have fully preached the gospel of Christ...Now I beseech you, brethren, for the Lord Jesus Christ's sake, and for the love of the Spirit, that ye strive together with me in your prayers to God for me"* (KJV).

It is unfortunate when we limit the ministry of the Holy Spirit in our lives to just speaking in tongues. Certainly, this prayer in the Spirit is absolutely essential, and I want to underscore that.

121

I pray in tongues everyday of my life. Indeed, on a normal day I will pray from 30-60 minutes in the Spirit.

God's Word and personal experience tell me that in doing this I am building up, or edifying, the inner person. However, the ministry of the Holy Spirit in our lives should — and does — go beyond this dimension alone.

The Holy Spirit's Ministry of Power

It is through the working of the Holy Spirit that God's power is revealed to the world. In Genesis 1:2 the Spirit of God is seen as moving or brooding upon the waters. It appears the Holy Spirit provides the power for creation's work. According to Romans 1:4, the Holy Spirit played an active role in the resurrection of Jesus. In Acts 5:3-5 the Holy Spirit seems to have been sinned against by Ananias and later Sapphira, and, in turn, He brings judgment. Paul consistently refers to the Holy Spirit as being the source of power in his ministry. He writes in 1 Thessalonians 1:5, *"Our gospel came not unto you in word only, but also in power, and in the Holy Ghost, and in much assurance..."* (KJV)

Here in Romans 15 the power of the Holy Spirit is seen in three areas.

First, the Holy Spirit helps us to *"abound in hope."* So many people live their lives devoid of hope. They have no hope that their situation will ever be any better.

I stood in the place of business of a brother in the Lord. He expressed deep frustration over his spiritual life. "Pastor, it has always been this way in my life, and it will always be this way in my life." He felt deeply that nothing was going to change. No matter what he did, it would not work.

Many feel they are totally locked into their situation. They see no hope for improvement in their economic condition. Domestic impossibilities seem to be the order of the day. Physical infirmity is accepted as being the only option available to them.

However, the Holy Spirit wants you to *"abound in hope."* The *Amplified* uses the terms *overflowing*, which is *"bubbling over,"* with hope. I believe Spirit-filled believers should be the most positive, hope-filled people in the world.

This is not a mind over matter hope, a psyching up of a person. I have not talked myself into this hope. I am not ignoring the realities which surround me.

Rather, this is a hope, a thought that things will improve, that has been placed in my spirit by the Holy Spirit. This is a Divine possibility for my impossibility. This is the chance of survival that the Great Survivor has given me.

I love watching the Holy Spirit put hope back into the eyes of hopeless individuals. I remember the Sunday night a lady in my church stood at the altar as the model of depression. Her shoulders were slumped, and her arms hung down in defeat. A few months earlier she had re-committed her life to Jesus. Her decision to do this was not applauded by the unbelieving man she had formerly been dating. She had indicated she would no longer be in a relationship with him, and that news had angered him. He had begun to make threats against her and her son if she did not return to him.

She would send her son to school each day with the question, "Would this be the day this man would make good on his threats?" Not long before this Sunday night service, she had left an evening church service to discover someone had been under the hood of her car and had jerked loose every wire they could reach. We were certain as to the culprit, but we had no proof. Just a few days earlier, she had awakened to the smell of smoke. Her garage was on fire! The investigation by the fire marshal made it clear the fire was the work of an arsonist. Again, we were certain of the culprit, but no proof existed. A restraining order had previously been placed against this man, but we suspected it was not worth the paper it was written on. He would do what he wanted to do. This dear lady had suggested to me she should buy a gun. I was concerned she was prepared to go buzzard hunting. I suggested to her that it was probably not the will of God that she blast this guy into hell and herself into prison. Now, she stood at the altar of our church. That night the Spirit of God fell upon her! Hands that had been hanging at her side began to be lifted in praise. She literally began to jump up and down and shout as the joy of the Lord filled her. Hope returned! She called the church office the next morning to report to me that she had actually slept all night through. Her hope had been restored. The inner peace was there again. You ask what happened to "Buzzard?" We really do not know. He disappeared, never to be heard from again. The Lord later brought a fine Christian man into her life. God blessed their marriage, and they served as leaders in their church.

Not only does the Holy Spirit restore hope in hopeless circumstances, but He also provides joy and peace in believing. Once hope has been restored, faith becomes a possibility once again. As faith begins to surge through our spirit, then joy and peace spring forth.

My life has been marked by great services. I remember a particular revival service where I watched this ministry of joy and peace occurring. At the altar the evangelist was on his face on the back of the platform. He was in another world with Jesus. Forget about him, he did not figure in the events that would follow. My father was as drunk on the Spirit as a person could get! At one point he decided to walk from the altar to the back of the auditorium. He used every square inch of that middle aisle. When he got to the back wall and leaned against it, he simply slid down the wall to sit there totally intoxicated in the Holy Spirit. However, the key man in this story was the fellow rocking back and forth laughing in the Spirit as he was sitting on the altar. When he was able to stop laughing for a few minutes, he observed he had no reason to laugh. He and his family had moved to our community a few weeks earlier with the promise of a job. However, upon their arrival, they discovered the job was no longer available to him. Since he no longer had a job, the house they had anticipated moving into was no longer available. So they were both homeless and jobless.

Additionally, he was facing rebellion from his offspring. His comment was, "I should not be laughing, I should be crying, but I cannot help laughing, I feel so good."

It was the ministry of the Spirit to bring joy and peace.

Thirdly, the Holy Spirit provides signs and wonders to confirm the Gospel.

According to Romans 15:18,19, the Gentiles became convinced of the authenticity of the gospel because of the signs and wonders which followed Paul. Miracles are nothing less than the mighty power of the Holy Spirit being revealed. Some struggle mightily to master the formula, to muster up sufficient faith. May I suggest what we must have is the simple anointing of the Holy Spirit. When we tap into the source of power, then things happen.

We must understand our total reliance upon Him. When we get less of us and more of Him, then things begin to happen. I have struggled to do it in my ability to only see the difference when the Spirit does the work. I have often said the secret in receiving the baptism in the Holy Spirit is surrender. One does not receive the Spirit by struggle. Rather, we receive because we surrender to Him.

The Holy Spirit's Ministry of Sanctification

Paul's desire is that the Gentiles might become acceptable to God as they are *"sanctified by the Holy Ghost."* Sanctification must not be thought of as a spiritual dirty word, as something impossible to attain. For us to be sanctified means primarily to be set apart from the world and consecrated to God. This is always a beautiful, holy thing.

It is the desire of the Holy Spirit to sanctify you. He wants to lead you into a deeper and deeper consecration to God. As this happens He also wants to lead you into a greater separation from the world—a getting the sin out of our lives. Genuine holiness of life is a concern of the Spirit. It seems to be one of His Words to the church today.

125

Here is the balance I somehow want us to hear. I do not want you to live under condemnation, but God wants us to not live in sin, either. Revival preaching will include the message of sanctification and repentance. I want the Spirit to make us very uncomfortable with sin.

There is a deep repentance from sin that the world, that is the sinner, needs to hear, but there is also a deep repentance toward and revulsion of sin that must happen to the believer.

One of the results of revival was expressed by a staff pastor who observed to me, "We have never seen our people living at this level of holiness."

The Holy Spirit's Ministry of Love

As Paul beseeches the Romans for their prayer support, he does it on the basis of Jesus' sake and the love of the Spirit. The Holy Spirit is interested in building our relationships. He will supply the love that builds the body, for Romans 5:5 promises us, *"...the love of God is shed abroad in our hearts by the Holy Ghost which is given unto us."* He will supply the love, but we must supply the willing spirit.

This ministry of love will work miracles among us. The Holy Spirit has helped me to love people whose actions I detested, and this brought miracles to pass.

She sat across from my desk when I was pastoring a church. She had been attending the church for a few months. She confessed to me that just recently, she had had an abortion. She really did not know who the father of the baby was. She had been with too many men on too many different nights. She was singing in the choir on Sunday and visiting the night spots in our town at night.

"I did not think it was wrong until I had the abortion." However, once the abortion had been performed, she felt the guilt of her sin.

I shared the following with her, "I am unalterably opposed to immorality. I am unalterably opposed to abortion. I am

126

unalterably committed to you. If you will let us, we are going to help you."

The words of Jesus from John 8:11 were very important. *"Neither do I condemn thee: go, and sin no more"* (KJV). A woman had been dragged before Jesus with accusations she had been caught in an adulterous act. Her guilt was without doubt. The religious leaders were prepared to stone her to death and hoped to trap Jesus into breaking the law of Moses or into turning off His followers. His response gave her hope and challenged the wicked scheme of His opponents without violating the law of Moses, of which by the way, He was the true author. Forgiveness was extended, but a change in lifestyle was going to be required.

The Sunday morning following my conversation with the lady in my office found her in the service. She voluntarily refrained from singing in the choir that day, so that was not a bridge that needed crossing. During prayer time she made her way to the altar, where she indicated she was ready to repent of her sin and turn to the Lord. He met her that day at the altar.

Had the Holy Spirit not helped me to love her on Thursday, I believe that Sunday miracle would not have happened. I want to make a couple of things absolutely clear. Her sin was wrong. I would never excuse sin, but Jesus still loved her. He wanted to minister to her, and His love for her was given to me by the Holy Spirit.

What is the ministry you need from the Holy Spirit today?

Some stand in need of the hope He brings. Some stand in need of His joy. Still others need an expression of His power. His commitment to minister to you actually exceeds your awareness of that need in your life.

Some are in the need of a sanctifying cleansing work of the Holy Spirit. You have been to the Cross for salvation, but there is yet more you need. You are on your way to Heaven, but there is still way too much of the gunk of the world in your life. Will you allow the Spirit to take deeper His work in your life?

I invite you to pray with me the following prayer.

"Jesus, I admit I have sinned. I want to repent, that is I want to turn away from my sin. Jesus, I want to ask You to forgive me for my sin. I have hurt You. I have hurt others. I have hurt myself. I am sorry. I ask You to forgive me. I believe You are the Son of God. I believe You came to this earth from heaven. I believe You were born of a virgin birth. I invite You into my life. I ask You to wash away my sin with Your blood. I believe what You said in John 1:12, if I would receive You I would become a child of God. I receive you now."

If you have prayed that prayer and surrendered your life to Jesus I would love to hear about it. You can email me at mikliven@aol.com, or go to mikelivengoodministries.com and share your story there by going to the contact page.

After our encounter with God at the Pensacola Outpouring in 1996, we walked into a season of the greatest revivals we had ever personally been involved with. I tell that story in my book, "The Glory Factor." During the first several years of revival, salvation and sanctification dominated my preaching. Repentance was huge. Let's get the sin out of our lives. However, revival preaching is not limited to salvation preaching. Messages on the manifest Presence of God became extremely important, as well. My aforementioned book, "The Glory Factor" and its sequel, "The Wow Factor," deal a lot with that subject. In this chapter I am going to share a message that emphasize this aspect of revival and its preaching.

CHAPTER THIRTEEN

I saiah 64:1-5, *"Oh that thou wouldest rend the heavens, that thou wouldest come down, that the mountains might flow down at thy presence, as when the melting fire burneth, the fire causeth the waters to boil, to make thy name known to thine adversaries, that the nations may tremble at thy presence! When thou didst terrible things which we looked not for, thou camest down, the mountains flowed down at thy presence. For since the beginning of the world men have not heard, nor perceived by the ear, neither hath the eye seen, O God, beside thee, what he hath prepared for him that waiteth for him. Thou meetest him that rejoiceth and worketh righteousness, those that remember thee in thy ways: behold, thou art wroth; for we have sinned: in those is continuance, and we shall be saved"*(KJV).

KEYS TO ATTRACTING THE PRESENCE OF GOD

One author describes revival as a community "saturated with the Presence of God." Indeed, the manifest Presence of God

129

appears to be one of the constants in the revivals of antiquity. Not only is this true historically, but my personal experience speaks to the same.

It seems to me that the manifest Presence of God could be viewed as the revival itself. The goal of revival could be seen as us knowing and walking in the awareness of His glorious Presence. Certainly, history suggests the manifest Presence of God is that which brings revival. For example, in the days of Charles Finney, it was the manifest Presence of God that would come to a city that was often a key to many in the city coming to Jesus.

The coming of the manifest Presence of God to a city has incredible implications and impact, but let me personalize this message. What are the benefits you can expect in your personal life when you have had an encounter with the manifest Presence of God? While the following is not exhaustive, let me suggest five things you will likely experience.

Benefits of an Encounter with the Manifest Presence of God

One of the great chapters connected to the manifest Presence of God is Exodus 33. This chapter was pivotal in my personal journey with the Lord. The Lord gives to Moses a promise of angelic presence and power as the people of Israel prepare to cross into their promised land. However, the Lord indicates that while they will experience His provision, they will not know His Presence because they are a *"stiff-necked people"* (KJV). Moses leads the people into repentance, and he indicated the accompaniment of the angels was not enough. I am challenged by the language of 33:15, *"if thy presence go not with me, carry us not up hence"* (KJV). May I say His face is more important than His hand?

Just prior to this statement by Moses, the LORD had affirmed His intention of going personally with the children of Israel, *"My Presence shall go with thee, and I will give thee rest"* (33:14 KJV).

Let's pause a moment at the word *rest*. His Presence would bring rest. One of the meanings of the Hebrew word includes the thought of *dwell*. Among the promises being given to these wanderers was that God would give them the land of promise. They would have a place to dwell or to live in.

But let me stay with our primary understanding of rest. The tangible Presence of God will bring rest to your spirit. The tangible Presence of God will bring rest to your soul. When His Presence invades your space, often there is a peace and inner quiet that comes with it. When His Presence comes, He often gives us an invitation to let go and lay back in Him. The soothing His Presence brings to our ruffled spirits must be experienced to really be understood.

On a side note, when people have an encounter with the Lord that we often call being "slain in the Spirit" where they are unable to stand and simply find themselves on the floor, they will often observe they experience an incredible rest. My eighteen-year-old son, who probably weighed all of 135 pounds, laid his hands on a man whose 6'5" frame probably weighed in at 240 pounds. The man ended up on the floor. Later, he observed three things. First, he observed, "That young man could not push me to the ground." Second, he observed, "I have a back problem, and I cannot lie down." Third, "I have never felt such a sense of rest and peace come over me as I did when that Presence came."

A second benefit you will encounter is the joy of the LORD. Psalm 16:11 declares, *"Thou wilt show me the path of life: in thy presence is fullness of joy; at thy right hand there are pleasure for evermore"* (KJV). But what is joy? The thesaurus in my computer dictionary uses these types of words, *delight, great pleasure, jubilation, triumph, exultation, happiness, gladness, glee, exhilaration, ebullience, exuberance, elation, euphoria, bliss, ecstasy, transports of delight, rapture, radiance... cloud nine, seventh heaven.* Do you get the sense of the meaning?

This joy is not the response to good things happening around you. This is not joy because your bills are paid and everybody likes you. This is the joy of relationship. This is just the joy He brings with Him. This is the joy of His PRESENCE.

This joy can express itself in multiple ways. It is not unusual for people to begin to laugh as the joy of the Lord hits them. Others may dance! Some may act like a drunk. Still others may just smile.

That joy will bring strength to you, according to Nehemiah 8:10. Happiness is usually related to circumstance but joy is much deeper than that.

A third value to His Presence is the victory it brings into our circumstances.

Isaiah 63:9 declares, *"In all their affliction he was afflicted, and the angel of his presence saved them: in his love and in his pity he redeemed them; and he bare them, and carried them all the days of old"* (KJV).

Your salvation does not come because of what you do. Your salvation comes from Him. His Presence comes to live within you, and as a result you become saved. Your works do not save you. His Presence saves you!

Here, the angel of His presence is described as saving them. I love this verse. In your affliction, He is afflicted. That is identification with you. He is walking with you. He does not just know about what is going on in your life; He is actually walking through the situation with you.

But it does not stop there. He saves you. He rescues you.

Let me quote from the *Theological Wordbook of the Old Testament* regarding this Hebrew word. "In the NT the idea of salvation primarily means forgiveness of sin, deliverance from its power, and defeat of Satan. Although the OT begins to point in that direction, the majority of references to salvation speak of Yahweh granting deliverance from real enemies and out of real catastrophes."

I never want us to forget that it is His Presence that brings salvation, but His Presence also brings deliverance, liberation, and victory. All of those concepts are in this word.

I have watched the difference in ministering to those who are bound by demons when that Presence comes. I have watched the healings that occur when THAT Presence comes.

Yes, we must stand by faith on the Word of God. I believe that, but I also understand that when His Presence enters the room, victory becomes easy!

Psalm 31:20 reveals another blessing of the manifest Presence of God. *"Thou shalt hide them in the secret of thy presence from the pride of man: thou shalt keep them secretly in a pavilion from the strife of tongues"* (KJV).

There is a protection...a hiding place...that comes from the Presence of the Lord.

I am reminded of a service from my youth. The church was in the midst of revival meetings. The leader of the special music team made the statement, "I feel like I am in my feathered bomb shelter." He went on to describe the beautiful home God had given him, but he did not want to leave the Presence he was experiencing to go to that home. He felt so safe.

That Presence can protect you from the pride of people...from the inner strife you experience because of what people say to you.

Let us make it clear that you will never stop people from talking about you. However, when you are in His Presence and you are hearing Him tell you what He thinks about you, it really does not matter what others are saying.

Do you remember as a child saying something like this, "Sticks and stones may break my bones, but your words will never hurt me?" You do realize that you were probably lying to yourself? Long after bones that have been broken by sticks and stones have mended, a spirit that has been damaged by words spoken will still be shattered. However, His Presence will provide shelter for you.

Fifth, His manifest Presence will bring refreshing to you. *"Repent ye therefore, and be converted, that your sins may be blotted out, when the times of refreshing shall come from the presence of the Lord"* (Acts 3:19 KJV).

There is just something so significant about the refreshing the manifest Presence of God brings. This has been one of the greatest ongoing stories out of revival.

I have driven fourteen plus hours one way to reach the great revival in Pensacola, Florida. Within just a few minutes of being in that Presence, I felt so refreshed. I have preached revival meetings where I was so exhausted, but then that Presence would come, and everything changed.

A young lady approached me after the altar service in an extended meeting to ask me if I would be willing to come and speak to her youth group. I indicated to her I would be open to that, but that I worked through pastors, so I would need her pastor to contact me. What I did not know was her father was the pastor of a church! The next morning he contacted me. Would we come and speak to their youth? I agreed, and a date for the next week was set. The night we agreed to was to be a rest night after speaking for 17 straight nights in a revival. As we were driving to the meeting, I indicated to my wife that I was crazy to have accepted this invitation because I was so tired, I felt like my eyes were crossing. As we walked toward the door of the house where 40 or more people had crammed into a living room, we could hear worship. I began to feel refreshed. After speaking for a few moments, I gave a salvation altar call, and a dozen or so young people responded. I started to pray for them when we experienced an explosion of the Presence of God. In about three minutes' time, all 40 plus people were "out in the Spirit." Linda and I just stood there gob-smacked by His Presence that had just entered the room. We immediately were totally refreshed!

We have been asked how we can maintain the traveling schedule we have lived with for many years. The answer is more complicated than time or space permits me to share, but the manifest Presence of God helps us to not be overcome with burnout. Yes, we get tired physically, but we are not tired emotionally because of that Presence.

What is it that Attracts God to a Particular Person…Church…City?

What is it that attracts God to a particular person…church…city?

In the great revival of the early 1900s, centered in Wales, Evan Roberts often prayed Isaiah 64 as he sought God for revival. His prayer was for God to *"rend the heavens and come down"* (KJV).

I submit that in Isaiah 64 are four things that seem to attract the manifest Presence of God. Those four words come through in both the KJV and the NAS. To me they are: righteousness… rejoice… waiting…remembers.

He meets with him who *"rejoices in doing righteousness"* (KJV). Several years ago, George Otis and the Transformation team shared the stories of several communities who were experiencing some level of city transformation. Holiness (righteousness) seemed to be one of the common factors in each city that was attracting the Presence of God. This was not a holiness manifested by a sinful city, but a holiness walked out by the church. In the Old Testament, the offering of consecration was offered before the fire of God fell in Leviticus 9.

Perhaps, I should pause here to explain that human righteousness has two aspects to it. First, there is imputed righteousness. This is the righteousness that is given to us by God Himself. This is a standing in right relationship with God because of what Jesus has done. Second, Corinthians 5:21 is the classic verse on this, *"For he hath made him to be sin for us, who knew no sin; that we might be made the righteousness of God in him"* (KJV).

The second dimension of righteousness is applied or practical righteousness. This has to do with our conduct. The righteousness we have been given becomes the righteousness we are living.

I read in 1 John 3:7, *"Little children, let no man deceive you: he that doeth righteousness is righteous, even as he is righteous"* (KJV). Heaven's citizenship does impact earthly conduct.

I have an increasing urgency in my spirit over this issue of personal holiness. I believe it is essential if we are going to carry the Presence of God.

The second key word is the word *rejoices*. Psalm 22:3 the KJV declares that God inhabits the praises of His people. Experience suggests that many of the most awesome times we have had with the manifest Presence of God have come as a response to our worship of Him. Have you found that to be so?

Perhaps we cannot overstate the importance of *worship*. Someone said that preachers will be unemployed in heaven, but worship leaders will have a job.

My wife and I were driving through northern Alabama, making up songs of worship to the LORD. Our songs will never make the top 40. Bethel has not contacted me to ask about publishing what we were singing, but it seemed our worship touched the heart of God. Somewhere around 2:00 a.m., the manifest Presence of God filled our truck. I was glad Linda was driving because the tears were pouring down my face, and I was having a difficult time seeing. I do not know if I had ever felt the Presence of God in a more intense way than I did at that moment. It seemed to me that I heard the Spirit of God ask me what He could do for me. It felt like a "blank check" moment. I felt like He was saying whatever I asked for, He was prepared to give me. The moment was huge. I told Him I felt inadequate to answer. The offer was too big, but what I really wanted was unbroken chains of encounters with His Presence. Even as I attempt to write this poor description of that moment, I am aware of His Presence. I tried to read this last paragraph back to my wife and found myself broken again, with both the memories of that moment and the awareness of Him in this present moment.

I have found a third key to be waiting on the Lord. Those who encounter the awesome manifest Presence of God understand you encounter this on His time schedule and not yours. When our hunger for the Presence of God brings us to the point where other things begin to take a back seat to that Presence and you lay things aside just for Him, you will be at a point where His manifest Presence will come. This waiting may come in extended times of intercession. It may come during times of worship. It may come in times at the altar. It may come literally in moments of doing nothing but sitting before and with Him.

I am not interested in long services for the sake of long services, but I am concerned that in our trend toward shortened, highly-structured meetings that we may be squeezing out opportunities for Him to come. It is not that He cannot come, but rather it is that He will not. Worship is not about me. He is to be the object of my life.

One season of my formative years included meetings where the leadership might take thirty minutes to make announcements. I am not campaigning for that. I have been in some services where I felt someone should have killed the meeting and mercifully put us all out of our misery.

I heard a former president of my alma mater describe old-time Pentecostals as people of the Presence. For them, church was not measured by the clock on the wall. Rather, it was measured by the manifestation of His Presence. They would come worship, wait until that manifest Presence came, and He ministered as it pleased Him. If that took three hours, they would wait. If that took forty-five minutes, they would enjoy Him, and then go home.

Waiting may involve time, but it probably involves a mindset even more.

Scripture uses the word *remember*. This may include meditation on His Word or His Work. Another concept that is finding a lot of acceptance today is the testimony. There is great value in the story. Have you ever sat with a group and just told stories of what Jesus has done? Have you ever noticed how soon He seems to join the conversation?

If I may reflect again regarding what I wrote just a few paragraphs ago, I will observe that in remembering that moment on the Alabama interstate highway stirred up something.

I am aware I have become famous or infamous for revival stories. I tell stories for more than one reason. Jesus told them.

Most people enjoy them. Sometimes they bring the wandering mind of the listener back to the moment. Stories are like windows that let the light in. Truth becomes clothed in skin. But one of the reasons I tell stories is that, as I remember, it is an open door for His Presence to walk into this moment.

My experience again and again has been that there is a connection between these four things: pure living, passionate worship, patient waiting, remembering His works, and the manifest Presence of God.

What Repels the Manifest Presence?

If these are the things that attract the Presence of God, what is it that repels it? At the risk of over simplification, let me suggest the reverse of Isaiah 64:1-5.

Genesis 3:8 describes what happened when Adam and Eve sinned against the LORD by disobeying His command. *"And they heard the voice of the LORD God walking in the garden in the cool of the day: and Adam and his wife hid themselves from the presence of the LORD God amongst the trees of the garden"* (KJV). The argument might be made that God had not yet withheld His Presence. I would observe two things. First, after God confronts them with their sin, He then withdraws garden privileges. They are cast out from His Presence. Second, I notice as soon as they have sinned, they are no longer comfortable in God's Presence. They hide from it.

After his sin, Cain is described in Genesis 4:16, as going *"out from the presence of the LORD"* (KJV).

In Leviticus 22:1-3 Aaron is warned that if his descendants attempt to carry out their priestly ministry with sin in their lives, they *"shall be cut off from my presence: I am the LORD"* (KJV).

Jeremiah also issues a warning from God to those living in sin, *"Therefore, behold, I, even I, will utterly forget you, and I will forsake you, and the city that I gave you and your fathers, and cast you out of my presence"* (Jeremiah 23:39 KJV).

138

Mercy is God's default mode, but if I continue to live in sin He will withdraw His manifest presence.

I would suggest that our busy-ness often causes us to miss that Manifest Presence. I can become so busy that I do not have time to wait for His Presence. Here is a personal confession. I have had moments of slipping into a church service with the secret thought that I hoped it would be a short service because I had other things I needed to do. Often these moments would happen when I was home from revival meetings. I went to church, but I had a lot of "stuff" to do while I was home. I mean, I thought this was important stuff. Usually, it was ministry stuff. Now let me be clear. There are moments where stuff does happen, and I believe the LORD knows that and works with us on that, but sometimes I can become so busy I do not take the time needed.

It is possible for a husband and wife to become so busy they do not have time for each other. We are aware the other is there, but we are not really aware of them. They are present, but we are not consumed with their presence. Some of that is the nature of life. But we learn if we do not "un-busy" ourselves and focus on each other, our relationship suffers.

God Almighty is always there, but are we too busy to really give Him the time He really deserves?

This leads into a closely-related reason we do not experience the manifest Presence of God. I would call this *familiarity*. We can grow so accustomed to His Presence that we assume on it. We do not take time to cultivate that Presence.

I do not need my wife to bow down and kiss the ground at my feet whenever I walk into the room. I am not so fragile, nor is our relationship so fragile, as to require that extremity. We are comfortable just being around each other. When we first started dating, we dressed for the occasion. We wanted to look good in the eyes of the other. We are closing in on 50 years of marriage, and we see each other in walking clothes more often than tuxedos and evening gowns. And we are good with that.

139

Still, there are times we just focus on each other. It may be a "coffee date." It may be slipping away from the crowds for a day or two. It may be a time of walking a New Zealand beach and holding hands. Recently, I took her away to a mystery location for a few days. Our relationship still needs to be cultivated.

God is not narcissistic. He gives far more into our relationship than we give to Him. It cost Jesus everything for us to be able to know the manifest Presence of God. Still, I must cultivate this relationship. I must not become too casual about my walk with Him. I must not let something precious slip away because it has become so normal.

This is a particular danger for the church in revival. At first, we are so caught up with what I call the "Wow" of His Presence that we cannot imagine ever going back to any other way of doing life. But sometimes, we become so accustomed to Him that we slowly begin to quit doing the things that attracted Him. We simply assume He will be there because He always is. We become too familiar.

I would offer one more suggestion. I believe flesh can become so offensive to the LORD that He begins to withdraw His manifest Presence. Flesh can occur in multiple ways. If the Spirit, through the Apostle Paul, warns the Corinthian church of the dangers of excess, I believe the same Spirit through the same Apostle warns the Thessalonican church of dead flesh. The Thessalonians are exhorted to *"quench not the Spirit"* (1 Thessalonians 5:19 – NIV), while the Corinthians are exhorted to put some boundaries on the events of their services (1 Corinthians 12-14). Indeed, we are warned *"that no flesh should glory in his presence"* (1 Corinthians 1:29 – KJV). May I suggest that is true whether it be Corinthian flesh or Thessalonian flesh.

I also submit those who genuinely encounter this manifest Presence of God will never be satisfied with less.

If I were preaching this message in an auditorium, I would probably be making the following type of call or appeal.

I would be speaking to those with secret or unconfessed sin in their lives. I would be making a call to repentance. I would challenge those who have allowed the yearning for the Presence to be squeezed out of their lives to repent for that busy-ness or familiarity.

I would challenge us to remember moments with Him that have been high water marks, and ask Him to renew our passion for these. Indeed, we would be asking Him to return to us as we return to Him.

I would open the altar for a time of waiting and worshipping.

Perhaps, today is a good day for you to do that. Perhaps, this is a day to repent and renew yourself in the faith so that seasons of refreshing can be released in your life.

When I started writing this book, I did not intend to include the material from this chapter in it, but as I prayed and contemplated the book, I realized that most of the book did reflect the revival preaching of the evangelist, or it reflected the revival preaching of the prophet. I began to feel it was important that I include at least one message that reflected more of the messages of the teacher. This is a teaching I have shared numerous times in extended meetings. Some confusion that occurs in revival can be somewhat mitigated with Biblical teaching. This message seemed to have that effect for many.

CHAPTER FOURTEEN

Hebrews 6:1-2, *"Therefore leaving the principles of the doctrine of Christ, let us go on unto perfection; not laying again the foundation of repentance from dead works, and of faith toward God, Of the doctrine of baptisms, and of laying on of hands, and of resurrection of the dead, and of eternal judgment"* (KJV).

THE LAYING ON OF HANDS

Scripture is full of great truths that have been abused. Tragically, great revivals have gone bad because people placed too much focus on one doctrine or one experience. Sometimes, Biblical truths have been pushed beyond a proper framework or Biblical usage. Doing this has caused much hurt to the Kingdom of God, and often, individuals have been hurt as well.

Because of these excesses, perceived or real, some preachers have avoided certain Biblical subjects. I want to suggest we must not do that. We must learn to separate the good from the

143

bad. We must not make the mistake of throwing the baby out with the dirty bathwater.

I was introduced to this danger in the first church I pastored. I followed a dear man who was a brilliant Biblical teacher, but most of us have blind spots. He apparently had seen the gifts of the Spirit badly abused. In his attempt to correct the situation, he appeared to have thrown the baby out with the dirty bathwater. The correction applied had led many in the church to be afraid of the gifts of the Spirit, and essentially all expressions of those gifts had ceased before our arrival.

Even though Hebrews 6:1-2 defines the laying on of hands as a foundational doctrine, it can still be a problematic issue for some. It would not be unfair to say this foundational doctrine has disappeared from much of Christianity. Within Pentecostal/Charismatic circles the revivals of the 1990s seemed to have brought this teaching to the fore again. Indeed, in most of the "revival" churches I minister in, laying on of hands is a standard procedure. Many have experienced great blessing as hands were laid on them. In some churches the meeting is not complete until people have hands laid on them. However, it was not and is not a panacea. Just having hands laid on you will not solve every problem, but there are many blessings promised in the Word of God to those who have hands laid on them.

If I were speaking in a church or at an event, I would indicate my desire to do a little teaching on the doctrine of laying on of hands, and then we would take time to pray and lay hands on every person who would like to receive that.

Scripture teaches the laying on of hands for the following nine purposes.

Parental Blessing or Patriarchal Blessing

We read in Genesis 48:13-17, *"And Joseph took both of them, Ephraim on his right toward Israel's left hand and Manasseh on his left toward Israel's right hand, and brought them close to him. But Israel reached out his right hand and put it on Ephraim's head, though he was the younger, and crossing his arms, he put his left hand on Manasseh's head, even though Manasseh was the firstborn. Then he blessed Joseph and said, 'May the God before whom my fathers Abraham and Isaac walked faithfully, the God who has been my shepherd all my life to this day, the Angel who has delivered me from all harm – may he bless these boys. May they be called by my name and the names of my fathers Abraham and Isaac, and may they increase greatly on the earth.' When Joseph saw his father placing his right hand on Ephraim's head he was displeased; so he took hold of his father's hand to move it from Ephraim's head to Manasseh's head"* (NIV).

Jacob laid his hands on the heads of Ephraim and Manasseh and spoke a blessing over them. There must be something significant about both laying on of hands and speaking a blessing over people. In the circles I grew up in, many were so afraid of both formalism and fanaticism that we probably missed something very good that the Lord wanted to do for us.

I ministered with a New Zealand pastor who laid hands on his five daughters and prayed over them every night. Even after they got married, if they were at his house they wanted him to bless them before they would go to their own homes. In one season of extended meetings, I became the substitute for him if he was required to be gone and my wife and I happened to be at their home. The girls would come to me and ask me to lay hands on them and bless them.

I would encourage you to consider making this a part of your family life. I would especially encourage young parents to make this an established routine. The prayer does not need to be long for the value to add up.

Transference of Sin To a Sacrificial Animal

Leviticus 1:1-4, tells us, *"The LORD called to Moses and spoke to him from the tent of meeting. He said, 'Speak to the Israelites and say to them: When anyone among you brings an offering to the LORD, bring as your offering an animal from either the herd or the*

145

flock. If the offering is a burnt offering from the herd, you are to offer a male without defect. You must present it at the entrance to the tent of meeting so that it will be acceptable to the LORD. You are to lay your hand on the head of the burnt offering, and it will be accepted on your behalf to make atonement for you" (NIV).

This command to lay hands on a sacrificial animal occurs again in Leviticus 3:2,8,12; 4:4,15,24,29,33; 8:14,18,22. The one bringing the burnt offering always laid their hands on the offering. Four different types of offerings are considered burnt offerings: sin, trespass, consecration, and fellowship (peace or thanksgiving). For the purpose of teaching on the laying on of hands, we will not get into the specifics of the different types of burnt offerings.

However, we will consider, briefly, the significance of the laying on of the hands on the head of the sacrificial animal.

The Pulpit Commentary, in its commentary on Leviticus 1:4, describes the laying of hands as "the most essential part of the oblation of the victim." Another word for *oblation* is *offering*.

The Biblical Illustrator observes that the putting of the hand upon the head of the burnt-offering, and the subsequent killing of that animal by the one bringing the animal, were both essential in the sacrifices of the ceremonial law.

Charles Spurgeon suggested four things were happening in the laying hands on the sacrificial animal. First, it was a confession that the one bringing the sacrifice had sinned. Second, it meant he accepted that his sin deserved to be punished by death but that a substitute could be accepted.

Third, and this is the part we are looking at, the laying of the hand on the head of the sacrifice meant transference. His sins were now being transferred to the animal. In some way, that animal became his sin. The animal was now guilty of the sin. I must understand this truth. Jesus became sin for me. He did more than take my punishment. He actually took my sin. The Holy Spirit drives this truth home again in 2 Corinthians 5:21, *"For he hath made him to be sin for us, who knew no sin; that we might be made the righteousness of God in him"* (KJV).

146

Finally, in the laying on of hands was identification. He became my sin but His death becomes my death or as Galatians 2:20 reminds us, *"I am crucified with Christ"* (KJV). He became your sin, and you became His righteousness.

Leviticus 16 describes the laying on of hands on a goat that was not killed. We read.

Leviticus 16:20-22, 30, *"And when he hath made an end of reconciling the holy place, and the tabernacle of the congregation, and the altar, he shall bring the live goat: And Aaron shall lay both his hands upon the head of the live goat, and confess over him all the iniquities of the children of Israel, and all their transgressions in all their sins, putting them upon the head of the goat, and shall send him away by the hand of a fit man into the wilderness: And the goat shall bear upon him all their iniquities unto a land not inhabited: and he shall let go the goat into the wilderness...For on that day shall the priest make an atonement for you, to cleanse you, that ye may be clean from all your sins before the Lord"* (KJV).

On the great day of atonement, Aaron was to lay both of his hands on the head of the scapegoat and put all the sins of the people onto that goat. The sins of the people were then carried off into a solitary place. The great teaching of the goats has to do with what Jesus did for us. He is not only seen in the goat who died for the sins, He is also seen in the goat that carries the sins away.

Ellicott's Commentary observes, "by this imposition of hands, and the confession, the high priest transferred the sins of the nation to the goat. He then turned to the people, and declared, 'ye shall be clean'."

Matthew Henry Commentary agrees, "the sins of Israel" were put "upon the head of the goat."

Jamieson, Fausset & Brown's Commentary agrees the priest would place his hands upon the head of the goat, and after confessing the sins of the people, he would transfer them to the goat.

In the laying on of hands as we pray for people, we are seeking to be the channel where the Holy Spirit can transfer healing, blessing, the baptism in the Spirit, anointing, gifts of the Spirit, and so forth.

As a Testimony Against a Person Guilty of Breaking the Laws of God

We read in Leviticus 24:14, *"Take the blasphemer outside the camp. All those who heard him are to lay their hands on his head, and the entire assembly is to stone him"* (NIV).

This is the story of a man who had been heard cursing God. All that actually heard him were to *"lay their hands on his head."* Then, all the congregation *"was to stone him."*

J.F.B. says the "imposition of hands formed a public and solemn testimony against the crime, and at the same time made the punishment legal." In the strictest sense then, the laying on of hands here was not a transference. Rather, it was a testimony and a statement that the penalty of the act was upon the head of the man who had committed the sin/crime. In one sense, they were identifying him as the culprit. The one who had the hands laid on him was the one who carried the sin.

Set Apart People for Ministry

We are more familiar with the laying on of hands to set people apart for ministry. Acts 13:2-3, *"While they were worshipping the Lord and fasting, the Holy Spirit said, 'Set apart for me Barnabas and Saul for the work to which I have called them.' So after they had fasted and prayed, they placed their hands on them and sent them off"* (NIV).

After fasting and prayer, the prophets and teachers laid hands on Paul and Barnabas and sent them away. The laying on of hands did not constitute the call. That had already come. The laying on of hands recognized the call of God that was upon these men. It is not improbable the laying on of hands may have released additional anointing on them as well.

1 Timothy 4:14, *"Do not neglect your gift, which was given you through a prophetic message when the body of elders laid their hands on you"* (NIV).

We believe a ministry gift was given to Timothy via prophecy and the laying on of the hands of the presbytery. This gift can be neglected, so we must meditate on and give ourselves wholly to the gift.

Finis J. Dake says "power was given by prophecy and the laying on of hands." We would call that transference of anointing.

Other scholars believe the actual conferring of the gift came in 2 Timothy 1:6, where Paul speaks of his having laid hands on Timothy. As Paul encourages Timothy to *"fan into flame the gift of God, which is in you through the laying on of my hand."* (NIV).

For the Giving of An Anointing for Ministry

Speaking of 2 Timothy 1:6, I suggest not only was a gift or office given to Timothy through the laying on of hands, but was also the anointing for that ministry.

This gift is a fire, which if not frequently stirred up and more fuel added, will go out. The Greek signifies to "kindle up the fire; to add fresh fuel." This is the only time it is used.

This fire of God within Timothy was received when Paul laid his hands on him. It would appear a gift or fire of God can be released through the laying on of hands by another person. Once the fire has been released, one needs to stir up the flame.

This is one reason many revival churches lay hands on their people regularly. They are seeking to stir up the anointing or the fire. Early in our New Zealand journey, I was having lunch with an Australian pastor whose church was, even then, on year four of revival. When I asked him how they were able to sustain the fire of revival, he pointed to the laying on of hands, with the observation they laid hands on people on a regular basis.

Healing

A sixth Biblical purpose for the laying on of hands is for the healing of the sick. We see an example of this in the ministry of Paul in Acts 28:8, where he laid hands on the father of Publius.

"His father was sick in bed, suffering from fever and dysentery. Paul went in to see him and after prayer placed his hands on him and healed him" (NIV).

A spin-off of this is seen in Acts 19:11-12, where *"God did extraordinary miracles through Paul, so that even handkerchiefs and aprons that had touched him were taken to the sick, and their illnesses were cured and the evil spirits left them"* (NIV).

The King James says these *"special miracles"* were wrought *"by the hands of Paul."* It may simply be the Scripture is saying God did these deeds through Paul. Or it may be saying that as Paul laid hands on people, great miracles occurred. The anointing of the Spirit on Paul was transferred to handkerchiefs and aprons, and many were healed and delivered when these cloths were laid on the afflicted ones.

I am sure it will not surprise you for me to announce to you there are more references to healing than any other single use of laying on of hands. James 5:14, seems to have been an established part of church life.

"Is anyone among you sick? Let them call the elders of the church to pray over them and anoint them with oil in the name of the Lord" (NIV).

For Blessing on Children

The patriarchal blessing of the Old Testament was carried on in the New Testament, as well. We read in Matthew 19:13-15, *"Then people brought little children to Jesus for him to place his hands on them and pray for them. But the disciples rebuked them. Jesus said, 'Let the little children come to me, and do not hinder them, for the kingdom of heaven belongs to such as these. When he had placed his hands on them, he went on from there"* (NIV).

Dake's Annotated Reference Bible says, "It was common among Jews to take the children to godly men for blessings and prayers." He goes on to say placing hands on children was an "outward form of blessing in both Testaments." Jesus practiced this. As His representatives on the earth, we, too, may place our hands on children and in His authority bless and pray for them.

I strongly encourage you to not discourage children who want to be prayed for. In one meeting I strongly encouraged some children to get prayed for every night of the meetings. Those meetings ran for seven weeks, and those children did get prayed for every night. To this day I think I have a special place in the lives of those children, who are adults with children now. During a time of crisis, one of those children, who at that time had become a young adult, reached out to my wife on social media. That touch of God that had been released or transferred onto their lives was still having an impact.

For Baptism of the Spirit

I am a Pentecostal preacher, and I will never apologize for laying hands on people with the expectation they will receive the baptism in the Holy Spirit.

The Acts 19:6 description of twelve men at Ephesus receiving the baptism in the Spirit describes it like this, *"When Paul placed his hands on them, the Holy Spirit came on them, and they spoke in tongues and prophesied"* (NIV).

The laying on of hands is not the only way people can receive the baptism in the Spirit, but it is certainly a very common practice. I have laid hands on hundreds of people, actually probably thousands, for them to receive the baptism in the Spirit.

It is not unfair to make the laying on of hands a point of contact to release faith for this gift from God, but it is more than that. Acts 8 describes a move of the Spirit in Samaria. Great healing...deliverance...joy...and salvation took place under the ministry of Philip. When the report of this move of God reached Jerusalem, Peter and John were dispatched to go to Samaria. *"When they arrived, they prayed for the new believers there that they might receive the Holy Spirit, because the Holy Spirit had not yet come on any of them; they had simply been baptized in the name of the Lord Jesus. Then Peter and John placed their hands on them, and they received the Holy Spirit"* (Acts 8:15-17 NIV).

151

I have seen over 300 baptized in the Spirit in one service I preached. I think more than one hundred have received it in a dozen different meetings. When I was asked if I had a special anointing for the imparting of the baptism in the Spirit, I indicated I believe this happened because I gave the Holy Spirit and people an opportunity to connect. I gave altar calls for those desiring to be filled with the Spirit. Probably 50% of the people who come to the altar will be filled with the Spirit that night. Some nights it is much higher than that. Let me encourage you, Preacher, give people an invitation to come to receive, and then lay hands on them. You will start to see the numbers increase.

For Giving/Receiving of Gifts of the Spirit

After getting them filled with the Spirit, let's believe God for more. I take us again to 2 Timothy 1:6, *"For this reason I remind you to fan into flame the gift of God, which is in you through the laying on of my hands"* (NIV).

Undoubtedly, the most controversial part of laying on of hands has to do with the thought of a transference occurring with the laying on of those hands. Certainly, this is a practice that has been abused historically, yet Scripture does clearly teach a transference occurs when we lay hands on people. It is probably less controversial if we keep in mind that the one laying on hands is nothing more than a channel through which the Holy Spirit flows. The giver of the blessing, healing, anointing, etc. is actually the Holy Spirit. We are not giving of ourself. Rather, the Lord is giving of Himself. Even when Peter says, "such as I have, I give to thee," he is really referring to the anointing of the Holy Spirit.

If we were in a service together, I would be preparing to give an invitation to come to receive the laying on of hands. We are not in such a service, but let me encourage you to do two things. At the first opportunity, have a trusted, anointed servant of the Lord lay hands on you. Until then, I urge you to lay hands on yourself.

Certainly, the laying on of hands in revival meetings has been a large contributor to that which the Lord has done. This is a book on the importance of the preaching during revival, but the impact of what the Spirit did when Steve Hill, John Kilpatrick, and Carey Robertson individually laid hands on me at the Brownsville revival cannot be overstated.

I close with a story from Lester Sumrall, the storied founder of LESEA and pastor of a great church in South Bend, Indiana. He shared this story in his book, *The Life Story of Lester Sumrall,* as told to Tim Dudley.

"In England I was privileged to make friends with that legendary giant of faith, Smith Wigglesworth. He told me about his life and ministry and the secrets of his great faith. He spent much time reading the Word of God, once issuing a challenge to anyone who could catch him without a copy of the Bible on him. At one point I asked him why I never saw him down or depressed. He said that when he got up every morning, he never asked Smith Wigglesworth how he felt, but praised God, danced before Him, and looked to the Word of God for His direction and response.

On my final visit with him, Smith Wigglesworth told me, 'I am going to bless you with my spirit.' We knelt and he placed my hands on his shoulders and prayed: 'God, let the faith in my heart be poured into the heart of this young man— and let the works that I have seen you do be done in his life and ministry. Let the blessing that You have given me be his. Let the holy anointing that has rested on my life rest upon his life.'

I learned much about faith from Smith Wigglesworth, but the greatest benefit of my association with him was the spiritual impartation that has remained with me and shaped my life and ministry."

A Final Note

As I was reading this chapter of the draft manuscript to my wife, she observed that over the years we have noticed a certain reticence or reluctance on the part of many pastors to lay hands on their people.

Certainly, they were not uncomfortable to do so in relationship to healing and, to a lesser extent, for the Baptism. We will lay hands on children at their dedication, and we expect the laying on of hands for those being ordained into ministry.

Yet, it seems many rarely lay hands on people just to bless, stir up, or transfer anointing into the lives of their people. May I encourage spiritual leaders to not forsake this foundational doctrine.